Witches and Jesuits

Each year the New York Public Library and Oxford University Press invite a prominent figure in the arts and letters to give a set of three lectures on a topic of his or her choice. The lectures become the basis of a book jointly published by the Library and the Press. Books in this series already published are *The Old World's New World* by C. Vann Woodward and *Culture of Complaint: The Fraying of America* by Robert Hughes.

Witches and Jesuits

Shakespeare's *Macbeth*

Garry Wills

The New York Public Library
OXFORD UNIVERSITY PRESS
New York   Oxford

Oxford University Press

Oxford   New York
Athens   Auckland   Bangkok   Bombay
Calcutta   Cape Town   Dar es Salaam   Delhi
Florence   Hong Kong   Istanbul   Karachi
Kuala Lumpur   Madras   Madrid   Melbourne
Mexico City   Nairobi   Paris   Singapore
Taipei   Tokyo   Toronto

and associated companies in
Berlin   Ibadan

Library of Congress Cataloging-in-Publication Data
Wills, Garry, 1934–
Witches and Jesuits : Shakespeare's *Macbeth* / Garry Wills.
p.   cm.   Includes indexes.
ISBN 0-19-508879-4
ISBN 0-19-510290-8 (Pbk.)
1. Shakespeare, William, 1564–1616. Macbeth.
2. Literature and history–England–History–17th century.
3. Macbeth, King of Scotland, 11th cent.–In literature.
4. Gunpowder Plot, 1605, in literature.   5. Witchcraft in literature.
6. Jesuits–In literature.   7. Tragedy. I. Title.
PR2823.W49   1995
822.3'3—dc20   94-14201

2 4 6 8 10 9 7 5 3 1

Printed in the United States of America

To the Memory of
Frank and Elsie Meyer

for all the nights we spent
reading Shakespeare together
till dawn

The male witch with his magic circle, wand, and robe. *From the Art Collection of the Folger Shakespeare Library. By permission of the Folger Shakespeare Library.*

Acknowledgments

This book began to shape itself in my mind during the early 1960s, when I taught Shakespeare in the night school at the Johns Hopkins University. In the early 1970s I commuted from Baltimore to the Folger Library in Washington while preparing three lectures on Shakespeare which I delivered as Regents Professor of the University of California at Santa Barbara. The third of those lectures—"Lady Macbeth and the Witches"—was repeated at several universities, including Yale and Notre Dame, before becoming Chapter Four of this book. I read for years with a view to expanding that lecture, but I had no opportunity to deal with the whole play until I was invited to deliver the Oxford University Press Lectures at the New York City Public Library in May of 1993.

I am grateful to both institutions—the Press and the Library—for their gracious treatment at those lectures, and especially to Sheldon Meyer (of the former) and David Cronin (of the latter), as well as to the staffs at the Folger and Newberry Libraries. In expanding the three lectures to seven chapters, I benefited from the expertise of colleagues at Northwestern—William Monter's deep knowledge of Renaissance witchcraft, Lacey Baldwin Smith's of Renaissance English history, and Mary Beth Rose's of Renaissance English literature. Other scholars who gave generous help are Leeds Barroll and David

Acknowledgments

Bevington. I could not take all their deeply appreciated advice (one sometimes disagreed with the other). Some rightly warned me that suggestions about performance, in Stuart or in modern times, are necessarily conjectural and cannot rank with other matters in their degree of certitude. Admittedly. But I risk such suggestions, since I try to consider Shakespeare as creating *performable* meaning, not just words on a page. I offer some conjectures *exempli gratia,* to show these meanings *could* be performed—not that they *had* to be done in any single way.

Contents

introduction

The Trouble
with Macbeth

If *Macbeth* is such a great tragedy, why do performances of it so often fail? Its unhappy stage history has created a legendary curse on the drama. Superstitious actors try to evade the curse by circumlocution, using "the Scottish play" at rehearsals to avoid naming it, *Macbeth*. Even great actors and actresses—John Gielgud and Glenda Jackson, to name just two—have been unable to make the play work. Some have hesitated to direct the play, or refused roles in it, from a knowledge of its dismal record.[1] Adaptations of it can be more successful than the original—Verdi's opera, Kurosawa's movie (*Throne of Blood*), Orson Welles's abbreviated film phantasmagoria.

Just what is the curse on *Macbeth*? Anecdotes accumulate about mishaps in the staging.[2] But accidents plague all forms of theater. Heavy scenery is moved hastily in cramped and ill-lit spaces. Actors fight careful but risky duels, often half-blinded by spotlights or atmospheric murk. Sniffles are passed around in the confluence of backstage, onstage, and auditorium airs, variously cooled or heated (or both at the same time). Actors get laryngitis; stand-ins forget stage business and confuse their fellows. Cues are mistaken. Props break.

Since many people, from stage technicians to financial backers, spend their whole careers in the theater, they are bound to die at some time—and no one notices what play they were connected with at the moment. But when Lilian Baylis, the legendary manager of the Old Vic Theatre in the 1930s, died, her troupe was putting on *Macbeth,* so people talked of the curse.[3] Laurence Olivier twisted his ankle on the opening night of his 1955 *Macbeth* and had to restrain the leaps essential to his interpretation.[4] But he injured himself in several other plays, notably *Coriolanus,* and nobody called *those* plays cursed.

The inevitable problems of any production have taken on special menace with *Macbeth* because actor after actor is frustrated by the seeming unplayability of the piece. Elizabeth Nielsen claimed: "No actor since Shakespeare's time seems to have made a name for himself playing the part of Macbeth."[5] Kenneth Tynan agreed: "Nobody has ever succeeded as Macbeth."[6] By critical consensus there seems to have been only one entirely successful modern performance of the play, Olivier's in 1955.[7] And even Olivier had failed to bring the play off in his first attempt (done in 1938, the "cursed" Lilian Baylis production).

Where failure is so common, it is important to see why the exception worked. Reviewers were disappointed, in 1955, during the play's opening scenes, usually the most successful. Olivier seemed to lack some of his normal energy—his patented kinetic jolt—in the "surefire" encounter with the witches, or in the scenes before and after Duncan's murder. This is precisely where Macbeth and his wife fuel each other's resolution in some of the most intense exchanges Shakespeare ever wrote.

But Olivier began to soar in the banquet scene, where the Macbeth of most productions starts falling apart.[8] Olivier's Macbeth, who made his low-intensity first choices of evil in a hesitating way, rouses himself to accept his fate heroically. Instead of cringing before the ghost's repeated apparition, Olivier manned himself to leap on the banquet table and run at the ghost, sword drawn, in an exaltation of defiance.[9] Some crazed enlargement of this Macbeth makes him grow toward his doom, climaxed with the frenzied duel that ends the play.[10]

However one judges Olivier's interpretation of the play as a whole, he had identified its real problem, the way it sputters toward anticlimax in most presentations of Acts Four and Five. Macbeth and his wife, whose interchanges are the best parts of most productions, are never seen together in those final acts. His wife, in fact, is seen only once, in the brief (but effective) sleepwalking scene. The play seems to dissipate its pent-in tensions as it wanders off to England, brings in new characters (Lady Macduff and her child, Hecate and her train), deals at tedious length with the question of genuine Scottish heirs, and substitutes the pallid moral struggle of Malcolm with Macduff for the crackling interplay of Macbeth and his Lady.[11]

Even Olivier did not make most of these later scenes interesting in themselves. But people sat through them with a sense of purpose, waiting to see what new mad heights Macbeth would reach in his climb toward heroic criminality. Olivier solved the play's problem by turning Macbeth into Tamburlaine. It was a very Marlovian reading of Shakespeare. It had the advantage of keeping the hero alive outside the claustrophobic whispering scenes of the first act. Better a cosmic hero than a closet drama. Even Tamburlaine is preferable to Raskolnikov. Actors like Gielgud or Paul Scofield turned the first half of the play into *Crime and Punishment,* and then had nowhere to go with the second half.

This explains why the adaptations of *Macbeth* succeed, in our time, better than the original play. They cut away or cut down all the inert stuff toward the end. Verdi's opera spends less time on both the final acts than on Act One alone (the murder of Duncan). Verdi excised the Lady Macduff scene, Malcolm's testing of Macduff, the dealings with the English court (with its king who heals by touching), and the Siwards (father and son). Kurosawa and Welles observe roughly the same proportion between a lingered-on first half of the play and a drastically reduced second half.

The effect of thus "frontloading" *Macbeth* is to shear away any larger social context for the protagonists' strugglings. Verdi was explicit about the intimacy he desired for the Macbeths, even in the extrovert form of opera. He chose to do the opera when he did because he lacked the singers for a larger dramatic ensemble.[12] None of his music dramas has so much sung whispering, to be done in a "hollow" voice (*voce cupa*).[13] The whole play is absorbed, so far as possible, into Macbeth's inner state—as it is in Welles's film, where surreal stones and caves are projections of his own anfractuous mental scenery.[14] "The inner truth is that these [witches'] shapes are himself—his own desires, his own ambition."[15] Inner truth—mainly Macbeth's but also his wife's—is what many people want or expect from the play. "Outer truths" fall away; they distract when they do not detract from the inner quest.

The result is a lopsided play, dead in the most embarrassing places, toward the end, where the action should accelerate and the interest be intensified. A frontloaded play is a back-crippled play. That is the real curse. Olivier overcame this structural defect by a personal tour de force. He wrenched the audience's attention out of its old patterns, redistributing the emphases, achieving equilibrium by making the first scenes less absorbing than they can be.[16] He made the "crippled" part of the play scramble and skip, overcoming its inertia with his own prodigious energies, harbored for this late explosion. When that individual feat is removed, all the faults of the play remain.

But are they faults? I shall adopt, as a working hypothesis in this book, the view that Shakespeare was not a bungler, that he did not fill the second half of his play with matter of no interest to his audience. How might one test that hypothesis? One way would be to look at the other dramas being put on at the same time as Macbeth (roughly, in 1606 or the 1606–07 Christmas–New Year's season).[17] If they contained similar material, we can assume that the material had some theatrical appeal, no matter how difficult that may be for us to understand. It is a separate question whether that appeal can be revived today. The first thing is to ask what effects Shakespeare was aiming at for his own audience.

Later civilizations might wonder why twentieth-century Americans were so interested in frontier mercenaries of the preceding century—in "gunfighters." If people in that future world could know only one or two westerns, this odd taste might be dismissed as anomalous. But if they were to discover that dozens of westerns were made together, the films' shared traits would help bring into focus what people considered appealing in the genre. This would not explain the variations that make great art of common plots—what separates, say, a classic movie like *The Searchers* from the latest item off the assembly line of Roy Rogers films. But no one could doubt, with the range of westerns being produced, that the figure of the gunfighter had great symbolic importance to mid-twentieth-century Americans.

So let us take the scene that most disconcerts modern actors and directors in *Macbeth*—Act Four, Scene Three, with the stylized long intellectual game by which Malcolm tests Macduff's willingness to compromise with evil. If we should find similar scenes in other plays being put on at the same time, we might conclude that they held a particular interest for those attending plays in 1606. We do find such plays, and in all of them there is an interest in the uses of deception to test loyalty, and in words as equivocal in their meaning.

The witches' cauldron scene, the necromancy, also embarrasses critics—by its length among other things, which encourages editors and directors to delete the Hecate speeches and songs of the First Folio. But what if we found necromancy scenes of a very similar sort in other plays of 1606? I shall argue that we do. And here is the most interesting aspect of this test: the same plays that have the equivocal-word tests also have the necromancy scenes. A *cluster* of common elements is beginning to emerge. This might seem odd or implausible if these elements were not parts of a larger similarity, in which they are naturally incorporated. *All these plays have reference to the Gunpowder Plot of 1605,* the overriding matter of political interest in the succeeding year, prompting sermons, treatises, ballads, pamphlets, and satires, as well as plays. All this literature shared common images and language.

If we were to see "sneak attack" used over and over in 1942, no matter what the context, we would recognize that those hearing the words could not help but connect them somehow with the 1941 raid on Pearl Harbor. In the same way, when we see words like "vault" and "train" (noun) and "mine" (verb) repeatedly used in the literature (in and outside the theater) of 1606, we have to catch echoes of those words' canonical use to describe what the Powder Plotters tried to do—blow up the entire government of England. The event and its aftermath—the trials of the Plotters, the rites set up to commemorate their discovery and capture, the elaboration of an official interpretation of all the surrounding circumstances—established the atmosphere in which people attended the theater in 1606 (just as surely as Pearl Harbor established the atmosphere in which people attended movies in 1942 and 1943). There was a rash of Gunpowder plays in 1606.

What makes a Gunpowder play? References to the Plot are one essential. These references must be obvious, although indirect (the condition of even relaxed censors' rules). But some larger themes are also essential. The typical Gunpowder play deals with the apocalyptic destruction of a kingdom (attempted or accomplished), with convulsions brought about by secret "mining" (undermining), plots, and equivocation. And witches are active in this process. When that pattern occurs, along with direct references to the Powder Treason, one has a Gunpowder play. The pattern occurs in *Macbeth,* as well as in these contemporary dramas:

John Marston, *Sophonisba*

Thomas Dekker, *The Whore of Babylon*

Barnabe Barnes, *The Devil's Charter*

There are many other plays, earlier or later, that deal with some of these themes—with witchcraft, equivocation, political apocalypse, tested loyalties, secret plots. Aspects of those plays will be looked at, where they are relevant; but they do not have the particular constellation of all these factors, presented at the time of the Plot and in the language of the Plot.[18]

Introduction

Macbeth looks like a different play when we consider it in this context, in conjunction with these other artifacts. That does not of itself make it a better play. John Ford's *The Searchers* is not a great movie because of what it shares with western "serials" or B movies. But at least we know, from the collocation with other westerns, what *kind* of movie *The Searchers* is. By historical accident, we have forgotten what kind of play *Macbeth* is; and before deciding how good it is of that kind, we must recover the kind. That will involve, at the outset, recovering the way the Gunpowder Plot filled and colored the popular imagination in its immediate aftermath.

This new context is bound to affect the way we judge modern productions of the play. A focus on the larger social drama of the Gunpowder Plot makes for a drama less exclusively centered on Macbeth and his wife—which means one less confined to the earlier parts of the drama. It is interesting to note that the idea of a "curse" on the play arose only after the Hecate scenes in the last half were excised. No one thought the play cursed when David Garrick acted in it during the eighteenth century, or Edmund Kean in the nineteenth. Admittedly, the text used then was "unauthentic" in ways that went beyond the Hecate scenes. But those adaptations (unlike the modern ones by Welles and Kurosawa) had strong second halfs. The question is: can we recover a view of the play that makes for a strong second half, without resorting to the kinds of additions William Davenant made in the Restoration period? *Macbeth* was once playable. If it could be made playable again, the curse would disappear. We would recognize that the curse grew out of twentieth-century performing practice (based on twentieth-century editing practice), not out of the play itself.

one

Gunpowder

dire combustion and confus'd events

How to suggest the scale of it? For a parallel we might imagine America in the 1950s, and suppose that a communist cell—made up of Americans acting under foreign direction—has planted a nuclear device under the United States Capitol. It is timed to go off when the President is addressing both houses of the Congress. All executive officers will be there, as well as all justices of the Supreme Court. The three branches of government will be wiped out. Every constitutional successor to the President will die with him.

But then, at the last minute, the device is discovered and disarmed. The President himself deciphers a clue that had puzzled the FBI and the CIA. The Leader of the Free World thwarts godless communism, vindicating the providential role of the United States in an apocalyptic time of confrontation between Good and Evil.

That is how much of the American public would have interpreted such events at the height of the Cold War. And that is the way godfearing English subjects interpreted the attempt on their sovereign's life and government in 1605, when a religious cold war existed between England and papal Rome. A cell of papists—the "enemy within" of that time, directed from Rome by skulking Jesuits—had trundled keg after keg of gunpowder into a vault under Parliament. A munitions expert named Guy Fawkes was discovered with the detonating materials, ready to ignite the fuse (train) when the King was addressing his Parliament, in presence of the Prince his heir and all leading members of his court. The Parliament—all the Lords Spiritual and Temporal, the leading justices, and members of Commons—would be consumed in a particularly horrible way. Gunpowder—considered the devil's invention, revealed to a friar-scientist—had the eerie and numinous reputation in the Renaissance that atomic weaponry acquired in the 1950s.[1] The relief of escaping this plot was tempered with fear that the hand of Rome had reached so far, had come so close to ending legitimate British rule. Though monks or friars had killed single rulers (a fact dwelt on in Protestant controversial literature), never had the destruction of a whole court or class been attempted at one blow.[2] But for a signal act of Providence, the Plot would have worked. Relief at the discovery of the Plot was tempered by continuing fear of the Plotters' ability to get that close to success.

Conflicting emotions ran high. Coming to grips with them posed some of the same problems Americans experienced in the shock after Pearl Harbor, or after the assassination of President Kennedy. It was important to address the crisis swiftly, so that panic should not ravel out the ties of trust and national resolve. The alarm of the citizenry had to be channeled into productive uses—as President Roosevelt used the anger over Pearl Harbor to drive war mobilization, or as President Johnson used national grief and guilt to pass social legislation affecting the poor and minorities. The government, in these instances, heightened what served its reconstructive efforts, and suppressed what would hamper those efforts. President Roosevelt hid the extent of damage at Pearl Harbor. President Johnson rushed through a report by the Warren Commission that did not pursue embarrassing CIA activities in the Kennedy administration.

In the same way, King James and his counselors promoted an official interpretation of the Powder Treason. Their aim was to achieve a quick consensus in the interpretation of unsettling events, so the nation would not be riven by random energies of doubt, or recrimination, or retaliation. Jack Ruby reacted to the killing of John Kennedy with his own reciprocating crime, and President Johnson did not want a nation full of Jack Rubys. Nor did King James want a country full of private vengeance-seekers initiating a reign of terror against Catholics. In fact, the Plot gave him his best opportunity to separate loyal and moderate Catholics from the mad extremists of the Plot. For this reason he had his propagandists stress that the Plot was less the result of Catholic theology than of a specific intervention by the devil, using only the most corrupt or malevolent elements in the Catholic community. For this effort, the isolation of Jesuits as the specific source of evil was very important. Other Catholics, lay and clerical, had some misgivings about the Jesuits' secret mission to England. The permanent discrediting of these troublesome underground activists could be one benefit derived from the Plot.[3]

The King disseminated his official version of the Plot in a flood of religious propaganda. The agreement of all these sermons, publications, and inspired pronouncements shows that they were the equivalent of a Warren Report, a government "finding" meant to quiet competing views, to heal the nation's wounds, to turn diffuse passion into focused resolve.[4] The key to the King's interpretation of the Plot was its subsumption into the apocalyptic reading of history that was at the center of religio-political ideology at the time.[5] The Plot was, on the one hand, a harbinger of the world's end. Yet, on the other hand, it proved that the end was not yet. The Plotters aimed at the government in England because it was (in James's eyes) the strongest bastion of the Reformation. If England could be defeated, Rome would have its way, and the foretold reign of the Antichrist could be initiated. But God showed he would not let England fall—it would stand as the champion of the true faith when the final show-down *did* come, as believers in the scriptural Revelation held that it must.

The King, as head of both church and state, imposed his views more directly and rapidly than President Johnson could in a democracy. The latter had to rely on slow procedures like the special Warren Commission examinations. James intended his reading of the Plot to become central to England's sense of identity. That is why he kept up a long campaign of indoctrination, to inculcate the lessons of the Plot as a statement of his kingdom's place in God's providence. The national character was at stake in the way the Plot was described and the delivery from it celebrated. The long history of Guy Fawkes Day festivities shows how successful the King was in this project. We can trace some of the stages in this quick response and long campaign.

1. On November 9, four days after the Plot's discovery, the King went before Parliament and gave his scriptural interpretation of what had occurred.

2. On November 10, just one day later, the Bishop of Rochester

preached an authorized sermon at Paul's Cross, repeating the main points of the King's address. This was immediately printed and circulated.

3. Sir Edward Coke, trying first the layman Plotters in January, 1606, and then the Jesuit co-conspirators in March, 1606, placed both prosecutions within the framework of James's theological argument. Most discussion of the trials has focused, naturally, on the evidence of guilt or innocence, so that the ideological assumptions of Coke are neglected. But for the long-term uses of the Plot, those assumptions were crucial; since conviction not only settled questions of evidence but imprinted an evaluation of the Plot's significance on the national mind. Quick publication of both trials' proceedings helped along this process.

4. The King arranged for recurrent liturgical celebration of the delivery from the Powder. This is at the heart of the Guy Fawkes Day festivities. The King attended church on each anniversary, to hear his favored preacher, Lancelot Andrewes, give a Powder Day sermon renewing the themes of the King's own first statement to the Parliament.

5. Issuing after and around the official statements, both popular and learned literature dwelt on the Plot and its discovery. Censorship of books and plays normally discouraged acrid theological and political controversy; but this ban was relaxed after the Powder Treason, to channel public wrath into approved reactions.[6] A torrent of printed abuse was loosed on the Jesuits, attacks on whom would divide (it was hoped) the Catholic community, leading responsible "old believers" to dissociate themselves from ecclesiastical regicides.[7] This literature united learned churchmen like Thomas Morton, one of the King's best apologists, and anonymous balladeers like those who published

The Devil of the Vault. Scriptural apocalypse in the sermons became lurid fantasy in the popular imagination:

> To see such royal and noble shapes
> Blown up i' th' whisking air—
> Here arms, there legs, diffused quite,
> Lie mangled everywhere.
>
> . . .
>
> Some, grov'ling, wallow on the earth
> In blood half suffocate;
> And every street be purplefied
> With gores coagulate.[8]

The plays produced in this time also echo the Plot, though censors laid a more restraining hand on drama than on other forms of literature because of the historic distrust of theater troupes and their playbooks.

6. When Jesuits, especially Cardinal Roberto Bellarmino in Rome, denied Catholic responsibility for the Plot, the King himself responded in several giant works of theology, and encouraged others to publish learned attacks on Bellarmino.[9]

To establish the terms in which the Powder Plot was understood, and its lessons proclaimed everywhere, we should sample these early stages of the royal indoctrination, moving from formulation of the official ideology of the Plot to echoes of it in the plays presented in 1606–07.

First, then, *the King's speech* to Parliament. James justified his scriptural approach to the Plot by noting that the Bible calls rulers "gods" of the little realms they are charged with (Exodus 4.16 and 7.1). The fate of James's English world mirrors in small that of the whole world.

The large world has two great trials to undergo—one past (Noah's flood) and one to come (the world's end by fire). In the same way, James had suffered the Gowrie Plot (1600), when his Scottish subjects tried to drown him in blood, and the Powder Treason, when the Plotters tried to end his life with the most cruel element, fire.[10] James's own "great and fearful Doomsdays" were meant to be interpreted together, since both fell on a Tuesday, the fifth day of the month.[11] (Number coincidences are signs of providential ordering in Revelation.)

The proof that God delivered James was the inspiration—beyond even his normal capacity—that allowed the King to divine the hidden meaning in the letter that betrayed the Plot. That letter, sent to warn a friend of the Plotters away from Parliament on the fifth, spoke of a "blow" to be "received" during this session of Parliament. A blow *struck* is the obvious sense. But the King, whose father died by gunpowder, had a mysterious hunch that "blow up" was meant, and he ordered a search to be made for blowing-up materials. This was a mystical experience his preachers would celebrate and elaborate on for years to come; but he set the theme for all their variations.

I ever did hold suspicion to be the sickness of a tyrant; so was I far upon the other extremity as I rather contemned all advertisements or apprehensions of [secret] practises. And yet now, at this time, was I so far contrary to my [trusting] self as—when the letter was shewed to me by my secretary [of State], wherein a general, obscure advertisement was given of some dangerous blow at this time—I did upon the instant interpret and apprehend some dark phrases therein, contrary to the ordinary grammar-construction of them (and in another sort than, I am sure, any divine or lawyer in any university would have taken them to be meant) by this horrible form, of blowing us all *up*, by powder.[12]

From this moment on, wordplay on the various forms of "blow" would be common in accounts of the Plot, or in references to it.

The King stresses that papists and Jesuits defend king-killing in general—and can therefore be separated from less fanatical Catholics, who should not be blamed for the actions of the zealots among them.[13] He has come to Parliament to prorogue it, sending the members back to keep peace in their districts during this panicky time. But he will call it to meet again when the Plotters must be tried. The culprits will be judged by the house they meant to destroy. As the psalmist says, "They fell in the pit they themselves dug."[14]

Second, *the speech at Paul's Cross* quickly reinforced the King's speech to Parliament. William B. Barlow, the Bishop of Rochester, gave the clergy's endorsement to James's theology of the Plot. Barlow, too, dealt with the matter in apocalyptic terms:

> I doubt not but, if it had been effected, that this whirling blast would have been unto our sacred king (so religious in his profession, so innocent from wrong, so clear in his conscience) as the whirlwind and fiery chariot of Elias, to have carried up his soul to heaven; and that God in his mercy would have made this deluge of blood as a *baptismum sanguinis,* a baptism of martyrdom, to have washed away our sins.[15]

This almost dares to border on sacrilege—the King's redemptive blood standing in for that of Jesus, streaming in the firmament like the blood invoked by Marlowe's Doctor Faustus.

Though the King lived, proving that the devil cannot remove England from the providential role assigned it in these latter times, no one should underestimate the diabolic malignity of the Plot, which meant to damn souls as well as destroy bodies. In a passage reminiscent of Hamlet's speech about cutting off Claudius's life in the midst of his sins, the Bishop said:

This devil of the vault contented not himself with the death of the body, but reached in his project at the second death, of the soul, by taking away many so suddenly, in their sin unrepented, with their minds unprepared.[16]

Like the King, Barlow made much of the word "blow":

. . . fire blown up, not down [like God's lightning] . . . in one blast, at one blow . . . with one blast, at one blow . . . this lawless fury had, with his blowing up, been blown in and over the whole nation . . . and blown out should they [virtue's lights] have been.

Barlow also began the long playing on Fawkes's name, which rhymed at the time with fox: "the sly fox of the wood to climb, the domestical usurper to intrigue."

Another theme that would become a staple of Plot ideology was that of "the pit they dug, they fell in." Some fleeing Plotters had put powder on the floor of their hideout, to dry it out. But it caught fire and blinded them.

[God] verified that speech of his son—Matthew 7. *In qua mensura* [with what measure ye mete, it shall be measured to you again]— retaliating their purpose with the effect of their own project, as if he would not suffer them to be taken till they were fired out of the house who would have fired us within a house—striking some of their eyes out with gunpowder (the instruments of our death).

This was doubly appropriate, since the devil's own instrument was involved: "gunpowder, which they say none but the devil, the King of the sulphurous pit, did invent."

Sir Edward Coke's prosecution speeches provided a third statement of official ideology-theology. At both trials of the Plotters, lay and priestly, the famous Attorney General was aware of the King's attention. It is plausibly maintained that the King was listening from an unseen spot at the trials—as he had wanted to interrogate the Plotters himself.[17] We shall see that the King fancied himself a kind of theological detective, shrewd at discerning real and feigned diabolic interventions in human life.

Coke founds his discourse on James's point made to the Parliament—that kings are as gods in Scripture.[18] He, too, puns on the name of Fawkes, refers to the backfiring of the treason when powder blinded the Plotters, and alludes to the devil's invention of gunpowder.[19] He introduces another conceit that would become a commonplace—that the Plotters meant to make others go up in powder, but *they* must go up, instead, onto the scaffold.[20]

But most of Coke's anger is directed at the Jesuits' perversion of the nature of language. Equivocation, as an attack on meaning itself, is a more fiendish instrument than gunfire for overthrowing kings. This makes the Jesuits apocalyptic bringers of "confusion" (the work of the devil).[21] The Jesuit superior on trial, Henry Garnet, was "a Doctor of Five Ds, as: Dissimulation [equivocation], Deposing of princes, Disposing of kingdoms, Daunting and deterring of subjects, and Destruction."[22] Number-mysticism was important to Revelation and language-as-natural meant that names of evil deeds were themselves evil. What seems to us a mere rhetorical gimmick was a serious theological argument to Coke.[23] Thomas Dekker wrote a poem on the Plot, *The Double P,* in which two Ps in the Pope's name (PaPa) stand for duplicity, just as the single P in Protestant stands for singleness of meaning, singleness of heart.[24] Dekker works out the contrast by pitting ten duplicitous champions of Rome against ten unequivocating champions of England.

Conscious of the eavesdropping King, Coke described at both trials the inspiration that allowed James to reveal the Plot:

> The king was divinely illuminated by Almighty God, the only ruler of princes, like an angel of God to direct and point, as it were, to the very place, to cause a search to be made there, out of those dark words of the letter concerning a terrible blow.[25]

He elaborated this description in the second trial:

> Their [the Jesuits'] secret intelligence was such as that it was impossible by the wit of man to be found out . . . and accordingly God put it into His Majesty's heart—[he] having then not the least suspicion of any such matter—to prorogue the [earlier] Parliament, and further to open and enlighten his understanding, out of a mystical and dark letter, like an angel of God to point to the cellar and command it to be searched, so that it was discovered, thus miraculously, but even a few hours before the design could have been executed.[26]

Lancelot Andrewes's Powder sermons continued the royal interpretive program. Preaching before the King in Whitehall, in the first of what would be ten annual sermons on the Treason, Andrewes said that the Plotters hoped to make November 5 a foul day, a no-day; but it remains God's day. "Be they fair or foul, glad or sad, as the poet calleth him the Great Diespiter, the Father of Days, has made them all."[27] This reference to the fair or foul day of November 5 was probably made within two months of *Macbeth*'s first performance. I do not suppose that Shakespeare is quoting Andrewes when he has Macbeth enter saying "So foul and fair a day I have not seen," since the idea of the fifth as a foul day that God turned back to fair was a common one.

Andrewes's apocalyptic vision of just how foul Guy Fawkes Day would have been, but for God's intervention, is not far from the popular poem *The Devil of the Vault*—"so much blood as would have made it rain blood, so many baskets of heads, so many pieces of rent bodies cast up and down and scattered all over the face of the earth."[28] But in fact, God made the plan backfire, "cast their own powder in their faces, powdered them and disfigured them."[29] And it was all done through the King. God "made him as Joseph, 'the revealer of secrets,' to read the riddle, giving him wisdom to make both explication (what they would do) and application (where it was they would do it). This was God, certainly."

Finally, *the popular literature* echoed and extended Plot ideology. I have referred to things like Dekker's *The Double P* and the anonymous *The Devil of the Vault*. Other poems and pamphlets will be referred to in the course of this book—things like the treatment of Father Garnet, the equivocator, in *The Jesuits' Miracles:*

> Then, of that troop, Cerberus their captain-chief,
>   Whose counsel did each secret ill direct,
> False traitor Garnet, that sole murthering thief,
>   *His* treason did *each* treason's plot protect.[30]

Most interesting for this book's purpose are the plays. I shall glance briefly at two, to be used more thoroughly in later discussions, before touching on some points of language in *Macbeth*.

The King's Men, Shakespeare's own company, presented Barnabe

Barnes's Gunpowder play, *The Devil's Charter*, during the post-Christmas season of 1606–07. In this drama, Pope Alexander VI, the Borgia Pope, makes a contract (charter) with the devil to destroy all powers opposed to his hellish reign in Rome. Though the historical time of the play precedes the founding of the Jesuits, the Pope is presented as a proto-Jesuit done in by his own equivocations with the devil.[31] The language is full of words weighted with Plot-connections—mine, train, lint-stock, plot, blow. Scattered throughout, such terms cluster in this thinly veiled description of Guy Fawkes (where I italicize the Plot words):

> I fought at Malta when the town was girt
> With Sergeants' Heads and *Bullbeggars* of Turkey,
> And by my *plot, mining* below the rampire
> We gave th' obgoblins leave to scale our walls,
> And being mounted all upon that place,
> I with my *lint-stock* gave fire to the *train*
> And sent them cap'ring up to *Capricornus.*
> Which, when the wise astronomers of Greece
> Prodigiously discover'd from afar,
> They thought those Turkish fiery meteors
> Which, with their pikes, were pushing in the clouds.
> The learned bookmen writ strange almanacs
> Of signs and apparitions in the air.[32]

The final lines recall the limbs "blown up i' th' whisking air" of the poem *The Devil of the Vault.* Or Lancelot Andrewes's "bodies cast up and down." Or Barlow's "parcel-meal" blown bodies. Or Francis Herring's 1606 Latin poem on the Plot: *dispergi corpora passim / Exanima*—later translated as:

> Their bodies batter'd, shatter'd, torn and rent—
> Arms, heads and legs flying i' th' firmament.[33]

This shows how the drama picks up and echoes tropes and terms common to all levels of authorized reaction to the Plot. Even Capricornus is a reference to the Powder Plot, since Coke emphasized at the trial that "It was in the entering of the sun into the tropic of Capricorn when they began their mine [under Parliament]."[34]

Another play of 1606 has special interest because it is by Thomas Dekker—Shakespeare's collaborator on *Sir Thomas More* and the author of the anti-Jesuit poem *The Double P*. In *The Whore of Babylon*, Dekker shows how the papal Whore plotted to kill Queen Elizabeth. This is a transparent way of showing how the Plotters tried to kill James. (Even in a period of relaxed censorship it was against the rule to present living kings and contemporary issues without some such analogical fig leaf.) Dekker expects his audience to be thinking of the Powder Treason when he writes lines like these:

> Good shepherds ought not to care
> How many foxes [Fawkeses] fall into the snare.[35]

Wolves in sheeps' clothing become foxes in fawn's clothes (2.1.27–28). A plotter fears "Lest, worn too long, the fox's skin be known" (2.2.2). There is even a reference to "devils in the vault" (1.2.176) —the customary description of Fawkes.

One plotter against Elizabeth forswears the use of gunpowder against her—that will come later: "An' if you kill / With powder, air betrays you.[36] "Train" as a synonym for the Plot is sounded repeatedly:

Close trains and dangerous you did discover,
To fire which you were pray'd.

If his trains take well,
They have strange workings—downward, into hell.[37]

The language of "blows," whose mystery the King unraveled, is here:

When mines are to be blown up, men dig deep.[38]

The papal Whore of Rome orders her minions, sent off to England:

Blow up, pull down, ruin all . . .[39]

I have begun with the least important aspect of the Gunpowder plays—their charged terms. More important things—witches and necromancy, Jesuits and equivocation—will be dealt with later, since they need more extended consideration. But the terminology is a first indicator of the atmosphere in which the plays were performed. Words like "train" and "blow" could no more be used "innocently" in the aftermath of the Powder Plot than could "sneak attack" or "grassy knoll" in the aftermath of Pearl Harbor or John Kennedy's assassination. In times of profound national uneasiness, verging (in places) on hysteria, these phrases became "hot," as if by radiation-contamination. Even "sneaky" was, for a while, a more seriously weighted term than it would have been outside the penumbra of the Hawaiian assault. "Lone assassin," or its components, took on the same temporary valence after the assassination of the President of the United States in Dallas.

So, when *Macbeth*'s first audience heard these words in Shakespeare, some ears must have pricked up (4.3.117–18):

> Devilish Macbeth,
> By many of these *trains*, hath sought to win me
> Into his power.[40]

At any other time, "trains" meaning "devices" would have no special overtones. But the other plays we have looked at show that 1606–07 was not just any time. There are admittedly fewer of the Gunpowder words in Shakespeare than in Barnes or Dekker. But we have to remember that the text we have of *Macbeth* follows its relicensing for a revival some years after its first performances. Censorship would have tightened up again, and topical references would have lost some of their power. Yet some traces remain of the language that seemed omnipresent in 1606—including that most potent term of all, "blow."

In a famously difficult passage, Macbeth expresses the fear that, if Duncan is murdered, cherubim

> Shall blow the horrid deed in every eye. (1.7.24)

This is an odd way of talking about the evidences of a crime; but it was Dekker's way in another play being put on at the time.

> An if you kill
> With powder, air betrays you. (*Whore* 5.1.43–44)

The horrid evidence of the Plot was blown everywhere in the writings we have been looking at—"blown up i' th' whisking air" (*The Devil in the Vault*), "blown in and over the whole nation" (Barlow), so as to "blow out" virtue's lights (Barlow). Earlier in Macbeth's soliloquy, he had referred to his planned act of regicide as a blow (1.7.4): "that but this blow / might be . . . ."

Another way evidence was lifted up into the air, blowing the truth into people's eyes, was the way the Plot's backfiring raised its devisers high on the scaffold. Coke had said at the trial: "by mining they should descend, and by hanging ascend."[41] That, too, would blow the horrid deed in every eye. The word "blow" is a pointer, here, to fears of the air-filling catastrophe, the planned Powder Treason.[42]

The death of the King is an apocalyptic event in *Macbeth*. Omens foretell "dire combustion and confus'd events" (2.3.58), and Macbeth says, of the crime's revelation (2.3.66–69):

> Confusion now hath made his masterpiece!
> Most sacrilegious Murther hath broke ope
> The Lord's anointed temple and stole thence
> The life of the building.

Confusion is the principle of the devil's reign, as order is of God's. Attendants on the Whore of Babylon tell her, in Dekker's play:

> On your brow, they say, is writ a name
> In letters mystical, which they interpret
> "Confusion." By Great Babylon they mean
> The City of Confusion.[43]

Confusion occurs frequently in the Powder writings—from Coke's speeches to *The Devil of the Vault:*

> Confusion with hell's horrid howls
> Denounces grim death's alarms.[44]

There is another use of "confusion" in *Macbeth*—at 3.5.29, where it means Macbeth's "damnation." This occurs in Hecate's speech, often deleted from modern performances—but see Chapter Two.

While Macduff has invoked Confusion, Macbeth—all of whose words over the deed *he* did are equivocal—says (2.3.95–96):

> The wine of life is drawn, and the mere lees
> Is left this vault to brag of.

Vault was the "grassy knoll" of Gunpowder writings. Macbeth draws an analogy; as heaven to earth, so Duncan's crime, in an upper world, to the lees in this underworld. Fawkes meant for the blood of the nation to be blown out of the upper hall of Parliament, leaving only the lesser breeds in the vault to inherit England.

One last aspect of Duncan's murder will be raised here, though it depends less on specific terms than on a whole cluster of words having to do with the penetration of secrets. James was praised over and over for his reading of the Plot's clues. But Shakespeare makes Duncan go to his death unsuspecting, with no alertness to the evil omens others become aware of. Duncan's *undiscerning* nature is emphasized by his own words (1.4.11–14):

> There's no art
> To find the mind's construction in the face.
> He was a gentleman on whom I built
> An absolute trust.

Nothing could be more at odds with the way James faced plots against him (not only the Powder Plot, but the Gowrie Plot, also commemorated in annual sermons that claimed he kept his head and baffled his assailants shrewdly). James *did* have an art to find the construction (construing) of deceptive appearances. He was a Joseph seeing through his brothers' lies, according to Andrewes.[45] He was like an angel looking through appearances, according to Coke.[46] He was like a wiser Priam uncovering the trick of the Trojan Horse, according to Francis Herring: "The shrewd king, sifting each point in his quiet mind said at the end of his reflection: These clues are not to be treated lightly . . . . ' "[47]

The proof that audiences would pick up references to a king's shrewd dealing with the Plot is in Dekker's play, where the attempt to shoot Elizabeth as she strolls in her garden is preternaturally anticipated by the Queen (*The Whore of Babylon* 4.1.69–71):

> It came unto me strangely. From a window
> Mine eyes took mark of him; that he would shoot
> 'Twas told me, and I tried if he durst do it.

This is exactly the kind of inspired hunch that came to James—but not to Duncan. Critics have often expressed surprise that Shakespeare's troupe would put on at James's court the story of a Scottish king's assassination. But Shakespeare went out of his way to show how different Duncan was from the picture of James being spread energetically through all the media just when *Macbeth* was first played. It is not enough to read *Macbeth* in isolation. We have to know something about what else was being said, sung, and staged at the time.[48] We have to be sensitive to language that bristled with the ideology of the period. So far we have just dipped into some of the scattered terms in that language. The larger patterns connected with the Plot—with equivocation, Jesuitry, and witches—call for ampler exploration. Which follows.

two

Witches

instruments of Darkness

Why witches? That question is often asked of *Macbeth*, whose witches have been treated as unwelcome intrusions in the play. But a larger question must be asked first: Why are there so many witches in the plays put on at the same time—by Marston, Barnes, and Dekker? Admittedly, witchcraft fascinated Renaissance audiences—it figures in many plays, directly or indirectly. In fact, there is not a single play by Shakespeare that does not have some reference to witchcraft, some metaphor based on it, some terms associated with it in a technical sense.

But the witches of 1606 are *central* to their plays, and they have a *political* role.[1] There are witches in every one of the dramas I am calling Gunpowder plays. Witchcraft was part of the ideology of the Powder Treason. It was not mere rhetorical flourish that made everyone from the King on down denounce the Treason as "diabolic." The Plot's hatching took place at a Black Mass, where hell's aid was secured by sacrilegious oaths and rites. Lord Coke at the prosecution said that part of the Plotters' crime was "the sacrament which they impiously and devilishly profaned to this end."[2] Lancelot Andrewes called the Plot "a religious, missal, sacramental treason," and added: "Hallowing it with orison, oath, and eucharist—this passeth all the rest."[3] Celebrants of such rites were, under Elizabethan law, witches, as we shall learn from Samuel Harsnett.

The Plotters' Mass was incorporated by Dekker into his *The Whore of Babylon*, where the Jesuit assassins, dispatched from Rome to kill Queen Elizabeth, swear an oath over the sacramental chalice. A Cardinal informs the Whore:

> Out of your cup we made them drunk with wines
> To sound their hearts—which they with such devotion
> Received down that, ev'n whilst Bacchus swum
> From lip to lip in midst of taking healths,
> They took their own damnation if their blood
> (As those grapes) stream'd not forth t'attend your good.[4]

So horrid was the profanation of the Lord's Supper to a regicidal purpose that, five years later, Ben Jonson turned Catiline's pagan oath into an anachronistically *sacramental* affair, to make it refer to the Powder Treason.[5]

Witchcraft is everywhere in Barnes's *The Devil's Charter*. The center of the plot is Pope Alexander's compact with the devil, making Alexander a male witch like Marlowe's Faustus. This pope sullies the Mass by having acolytes who are his boy lovers.[6] The Jesuits, too, were accused of pederasty with their students or altar boys.[7]

Charges of magic, idolatry, and witchcraft had long been leveled at the Jesuits in England because of their use of healing relics, icons, and exorcisms. Editors have known since the eighteenth century that

Shakespeare made heavy use of one such attack when he wrote *King Lear* in 1605—Samuel Harsnett's *A Declaration of Egregious Popish Impostures* (1603), which said the Jesuits' notorious exorcisms of 1585–86 were the acts of "devil-conjuring priests."[8] Shakespeare thus knew intimately one of the major attacks on the Jesuits as dealers in witchcraft. Harsnett describes the priests' "enchanted Babylonian chalice" in terms that would fit naturally into Dekker's play.[9]

The Plotters' regicidal Mass was a culminating act of diablerie, fully justifying Andrewes's claim in his Gunpowder sermon (delivered at roughly the same time as *Macbeth*'s composition): "Not man, but the devil, devised it [the Plot]."[10] And no sooner was the Jesuit superior Henry Garnet executed for the Plot than Jesuits began to claim miracles worked by his blood—further acts of diabolism. As a popular poem put it: "This wonder proved he was indeed deviline [instead of divine]."[11]

These aspects of the Powder Treason show why political witchcraft was so live a topic in 1606. Barnes's conjuror-pope, Dekker's papal Antichrist, Marston's hellish manipulator—all of them use rites and spells included in the repertoire of Shakespeare's witches. As the Bible itself said, "Rebellion is as the sin of witchcraft" (I Samuel 15.23, Geneva Bible). This makes nonsense of the claim that Shakespeare's witches are just emanations of Macbeth's inner state. The witches prompt Macbeth to regicide—the very sin the devil guided the Plotters to, through their oaths at a Black Mass. And that is only part of the witches' activity. They are busy about many things. Macbeth is only one item on their agenda.

Misreadings of that fact have led to confusion about Shakespeare's opening scenes. Some directors present the witches holding a "sabbath" at the outset of the play, or lurking in their coven's regular meeting place (some cave or shelter on the heath). But Shakespeare brings them bustling in from different directions, to exchange quick words, then hurry off again, summoned to separate errands by their familiar spirits—all this in only eleven Folio lines, the shortest opening scene in Shakespeare. They will shortly assemble again at this spot, when Macbeth comes by. If their only job is to deal with Macbeth (or reflect his inner workings), this scene appears superfluous. In it, they meet to say they will meet again before sunset—to meet Macbeth. If that is all they need to do, why not just stay there and wait for him?[12] Instead, they tell us (when they reassemble, later that afternoon) that they have filled the interval between their first and second meetings with a variety of tasks. One witch, for instance, has fetched a dead sailor's thumb out of a shipwreck.

Since they are pursuing separate labors, what brought all three together at this battlefield, earlier than their time for meeting Macbeth? What common business might they have there (aside from the later encounter) as their familiar spirits interweave their itineraries? No one in Shakespeare's time would have had any doubt about the motive. Battlefields were magnets for witches—for the same reason that shipwrecks were, or gallows, or prostitutes' lairs. They were all good places for collecting the most vital ingredient for witches' work—dead body parts, and especially dead bodies outside consecrated ground. All the body parts the witches name in this play— grease from a corpse hanging on the gallows, a whore's murdered newborn, a shipwrecked sailor's thumb—come from bodies either not buried yet (the gallows corpse) or not buried in consecrated ground (the drowned sailor), or unable to be buried in consecrated ground because unbaptized (like the whore's baby):

> Liver of blaspheming Jew . . .
> Nose of Turk, and Tartar's lips.[13]

Corpses on a battlefield are like corpses on the gallows—only there are more of them. No wonder witches flock to such rich pickings.

The importance of dead bodies was assured by the Bible's treatment of witchcraft. The Witch of Endor used Samuel's dead body for prophesying to Saul (1 Samuel 28.7-25). A flood of theological exposition came from this source, distinguishing diabolic possession of living bodies from the exploitation of dead bodies.[14] The latter use of bodies was called necromancy, prophecy by way of the dead (*nekromanteia*).[15] This, of course, is the act the witches will perform for Macbeth in Act Four. It was an act Harsnett attributed to the Jesuits (so common was the inevitable linkage: witch = necromancer). The Jesuits "do cog and coin devils, spirits, and *souls departed this life.*"[16]

Dead bodies had many uses beyond necromancy. King James himself wrote in his treatise *Daemonologie* that the devil sends witches "to joint [disjoin] dead corpses and to make powders thereof, mixing such other things there-amongst as he gives unto them."[17] The devil could also take semen from a dying man (or from a sleeping one) and use it in his couplings with witches.[18] Some believed (though James did not) that these couplings produced monsters or wizards— Shakespeare makes Caliban the offspring of a devil and the witch Sycorax, William Rawley made Merlin the offspring of a devil and a whore (Join Go-To-It). Thomas Middleton made Firestone the devil's child by a witch.

In any event, the use of dead bodies for occult purposes was felt to be such a threat that James, just one year before the Powder Treason, added to the witchcraft laws a decree of death for those who take up any dead man, woman, or child out of his, her, or their grave or any other place [like a battlefield] where the dead body resteth—or the skin, bone, or any other part of any dead person—to be employed or used in any manner of witchcraft, sorcery, charm, or enchantment.[19]

Thus it was very timely for Marston in 1606 to describe Erichtho's hunt for fresh bodies of the dead:

> From half-rot cereclothes then she scrapes dry gums
> For her black rites. But when she finds a corse
> *New* grav'd, whose entrails yet not turn
> To shiny filth, with greedy horror then
> She makes fierce spoil, and swells with wicked triumph
> To bury her lean knuckles in his eyes.
> Then doth she gnaw the pale and o'ergrown nails
> From his dry hand. But if she find some life
> Yet lurking close, she bites his gelid lips
> And, sticking her black tongue in his dry throat,
> She breathes dire murmers.[20]

That these were not just dramatists' imaginings, that such foraging through graves occurred in fact, we know not only from the King's realization that a law was required to stop it, but from accounts like this one, which describes a night foray by Edward Kelley, the dark associate of John Dee, Queen Elizabeth's astrologer. Kelley went on a conjuring errand for a man, along with the man's servants (sent to help with the necessary digging). In the first cemetery they tried, Kelley did not find a grave that was fresh enough for his purposes. So:

Kelley demanded of one of the gentleman's servants what corse was the last buried in Low Churchyard, a church thereunto adjoining;

who told him of a poor man who was buried there but the same day. He and the said Waring entreated this foresaid servant to go with them to the grave of the man so lately interred, which he did; and withal did help them to dig up the carcase of the poor caitiff, whom by their incantations they made him (or made some evil spirit through his organs) to speak, who delivered strange predictions.[21]

Kelley, had he been apprehended, would have been liable to the death penalty, as would his patron and the servants involved in this act—they were all, in the words of the King's legislation, "aiders, abetters, and counselors . . . [who] shall suffer pains of death as a felon or felons, and shall lose the privilege and benefit of clergy and sanctuary."[22]

Witchcraft was not just a matter of private concern, filling the law courts with complaints of hexes and love spells. It was a factor in affairs of state. Elizabeth's government showed enough concern when a crude image of herself was discovered that it called in John Dee, the master of occult lore, to prescribe protective measures.[23] This baffled plot against Elizabeth was described by Dekker in *The Whore of Babylon*, where a conjurer offers his service against the Queen (2.2.168–75):

> This virgin wax
> Bury I will in slimy-putrid ground,
> Where it may piecemeal rot. As this consumes,
> So shall she pine, and (after languor) die.
> These pins shall stick like daggers to her heart
> And, eating through her breast, turn there to gripings,
> Cramplike convulsions, shrinking up her nerves
> As into this they eat.

This is the "pining" spell witches were known for, the one Shakespeare's witch casts on a sailor (1.3.22–23):

> Weary sev'n-nights, nine times nine,
> Shall he dwindle, peak, and pine.

King James discussed such magic use of images in his dialogue.[24] Elizabeth was also attacked with hellish potions, including the magic poison smeared on her saddle pommel by Edward Squire.[25]

King James was even more plagued by political witchcraft than was Elizabeth. Most of the major conspiracies against his life involved witchcraft. In 1590 Dr. Fian used a "school" of witches to cast spells on him.[26] In 1593 Bothwell's rebellion led to an indictment for witchcraft.[27] In 1600, when the Gowrie Plot failed, magic formulas were found on the body of the man who tried to assassinate the King.[28] It is not surprising that the King should dwell on the dark arts that abetted the Powder Plotters—this was just a new piece in the old pattern of James's *psychomachia* with hellish powers.

There was, then, ample reason to be interested in the witches of *Macbeth,* entirely apart from the protagonist's mental state. The great scene of necromancy in Act Four, which helps delude Macbeth, reveals secrets to the audience about Scotland's history, about the future of Scotland's and of England's king. The spectacle of that scene is closely related to an almost identical necromancy scene in *The Devil's Charter*—and no wonder. The same troupe put on the two plays at roughly the same time with the same resources.[29] In Barnes's play, the Pope is seeking to know who murdered his son, the Duke of Candy (Gandía). He raises one spirit, which has to descend and bring up another spirit with the knowledge Borgia seeks. The answer is given in the form of a parade—an escorted "Candy" and his murderer, followed by another victim and *his* murderer, the devil guiding all four of them. The Pope cries, "No more!" and conjures the spirits down, with much theatrical business and sound effects. (The scene had opened with the appearance of a devil amidst "fiery exhalations, lightning, thunder," riding on "a lion or a dragon.")³⁰

Macbeth has three spirits rise, instead of two, and a parade of eight figures instead of five, until he, too, cries, "I'll see no more" (4.1.118); but the sequence and physical arrangements are the same, and so are many of the theatrical effects.

This brings us to the problem of Hecate's role in *Macbeth*'s conjuring scene. Barnes's Pope is his own conjuror; he is a witch who needs no witch helpers. But he calls on a whole hierarchy of evil spirits to find the right one who can seek in hell *another* one to make the required revelation. *Macbeth*'s witches are seen in the Folio text acting in subordination to their superior, Hecate, who has a "court" of attendant spirits with her.

All this offends those who want the witches subordinated to no objective order of hell, only to Macbeth's psychological makeup. Many critics express regret when the play wanders off, in its second half, to England. It is even worse, in their eyes, to have it wandering into a musical world of witch songs, with new characters like Hecate, and a new cast of evil spirits. The first witches were hard enough for some to put up with. Any more seem out of the question. The claustrophobic world of Scottish lore becomes mere pageantry, though a pageantry of hell.

Yet the text with Hecate is the only one we have, the one Shakespeare's troupe treated as authoritative when they included it in the Folio. If they felt it was inferior, why did they print it? Even those who doubt that the Hecate sections were made by Shakespeare believe that the play in the Folio was performed during Shakespeare's time, with his approval. Any earlier text was not considered worth retrieving.

Obviously, the taste of that time was different from ours. It should be remembered that the problem of performance, creating a myth of some "curse" on the play, came from the period when the Hecate scenes had been eliminated from performance. The latter half of the play seemed weak when the witches were treated as appendages to Macbeth's psyche rather than parts of a larger demonic world. It is interesting to notice that Hecate had a key role to play in Orson Welles's Caribbean *Macbeth,* set in Haiti and using voodoo as the equivalent of witchcraft. Once a *structure* of belief, with an *order* of forces, is called up, then it does not seem odd—it seems inevitable— that an opening into that world involves its higher potentates.[31] There is a movement in recent times to restore the Hecate scenes to the play, a movement discernible both in textual criticism and in performance.[32] This gives Shakespeare responsibility for his revived play, since he was, very likely, still the leading author of the company, and a senior shareholder, when it was relicensed.[32]

The Hecate scenes do have many signs of being added to the 1606 original—they introduce a large number of boy actors (chorus and attendants) available at some later private performance, and they use elaborate stage machinery (Hecate's car) of the sort that Ben Jonson and Inigo Jones used progressively at court. But removing the two Hecate scenes does not "restore" the 1606 *Macbeth.* These were probably not just added on to the former play, but *replaced* some demonic business having to do with necromancy. The parallel with Barnes's 1606 play shows that Shakespeare included a conjuring scene in the original (1606) *Macbeth*. This was not contained in his sources. The Macbeth of Holinshed has an assortment of "wizards," witches, and prophets giving him predictions and warnings. "Certain wizards" tell him to beware Macduff. A witch—not one of the three "Weird Sisters"—tells him that he cannot die from one of woman born, nor fall until "Bernane wood" comes to Dunsinane. No formal conjuring is involved.[33]

When Shakespeare decided to have these prophecies delivered in a formal scene of necromancy, he not only guaranteed some strong theatrical effects, but made an implicit pledge to his audience that he would involve devils higher in hell's hierarchy than the witches. We conclude this from the range of diabolic forces involved in the conjuring scenes of other plays. In *I Henry VI*, Joan La Pucelle calls up her familiar devils to protect her, invoking Lucifer himself as the Lord of the North, with much thunder and stage effects (5.3.1–24). In *II Henry VI*, the witch, Margery Jourdain, conjures for the Duchess of Gloucester, raising Asnath with the help of two assistants invoking devils (1.4.15–39), again with much thunder and lightning. Conjuring scenes have a similar solemn engagement with hell's personnel in Marlowe, Marston, and Dekker, as well as Barnes and Middleton.

It was never expected, then, that the witches would be alone in the conjuring scene. Act Three, Scene Five signals that a more formal affair is in preparation than the encounter on the heath, where the Weyard Sisters issued a prophecy but refused to answer Macbeth's questions—he would have stayed them, but could not. In necromancy, the conjurer gets binding powers to *force* answers from the devil. This is bigger magic, as Macbeth's great speech at 4.1.50–61 indicates: "I conjure you, by that which you profess . . . answer me / to what I ask you." Thus, though Hecate's chorus, attendants, and songs were probably not in the 1606 play, there is no reason to doubt that Hecate herself was there. She would put no strain on the number of boy actors evidenced elsewhere in the play.[34] An expectation that she would appear is signaled in Macbeth's earlier invocations of her—at 2.1.52 ("witchcraft celebrates / Pale Hecate's offerings") and 3.2.41 ("ere to black Hecate's summons . . . ").

Thus the Hecate scenes we now have—added as new resources came available for a relicensed play—stand closer to the thrust and import of what Shakespeare wrote in 1606 than does a play stripped of all supernatural "machinery" except the witches.

Even the revised text makes good sense. When Hecate, in her first appearance, rebukes the witches for letting Macbeth be "wayward" (3.5.11), this reflects diabolic anxiety that the compact is not secure. As we shall see, Macbeth has not given his soul over to the devil until he commits the formal act of witchcraft involved in his participation at the necromantic rites.

The Folio's "Weyard Sisters" may reflect Shakespeare's belief that they too, are "Wayward"—so Thomas Heywood thought when he made his Scottish witches "Wayward Sisters."[35] Higher devils rebuke lower ones for not "sticking to the program" in other plays—e.g., for showing the kind of pity that Mephistopheles expresses for Faustus.[36] Critics have said that Hecate has no cause for grievance with the witches, since Macbeth plunged quickly into murder to gain a throne and has already murdered Banquo in order to retain it. But Hecate wants Macbeth to give his soul over in a formal way, as Rome's rulers are bound by pact in Dekker's and Barnes's dramas, the other Gunpowder plays. Macbeth must tear up his "Great Bond" (3.2.49) to "take a bond of fate" (4.1.84).[37] Hecate presses this business forward, since it "shall draw him on to his confusion" (3.5.29). When she says that security will prove Macbeth's greatest enemy, modern editors think she is luring Macbeth into a false *sense* of security. But security in witch scenes has a more sinister import. It refers to the bond, the security, enacted by a compact with the devil. In *Doctor Faustus*, for instance, Mephistopheles tells Faustus:

> But now thou must bequeath it [his soul] solemnly
> And write a deed of gift with thine own blood.
> For that security craves Lucifer.[38]

This gives greater weight to Hecate's words in *Macbeth* (3.5.32–33):

> And you all know security
> Is mortals' chiefest enemy.

The enemy of man is speaking through his agent.[39]

Hecate's appearance in Act Four, Scene One has been criticized as stuck uselessly onto the scene's action. First she appears to give her approval of the potion made by the witches, and to add her own charm with a fairy round and song. Then she revives Macbeth's spirits after his vision of the successors to the Scottish crown. The latter action is especially jarring for those who interpret this scene from within Macbeth's psychology. Hecate actually says, at this juncture, "Come sisters, cheer we up his sprites" (4.1.127).

But bringing in the higher powers to preside over a scene is not unusual in demonic plays. Lucifer and Beelzebub appear, but say nothing, when Faustus conjures.[40] Asnath (a protective anagram for Satan) appears in *II Henry VI*, and lower devils run errands for Lucifer, who comes to take the Pope's soul, in Barnes's *The Devil's Charter*. In *Macbeth*, where appeal is made to the *art* the witches practise (4.1.50), Hecate, as self-proclaimed mistress of that art rightly presides. She tells the witches *she* is "the mistress of your charm," come to vindicate "the glory of our art." Her "great business," working toward a "fatal end," will accomplish Macbeth's "confusion" by way of a "security" (3.5.6–33).

As for the cheering of Macbeth after the vision of future kings, it should be remembered that the witches did not want to show him that dispiriting vision. Macbeth has used conjuring power to *force* knowledge out of devils—the *quid pro quo* given mortals in their traffic with the lower world. Mephistopheles shows similar reluctance to answer some of Faustus's questions, but must submit. After the blow the vision gives to Macbeth's hopes (seeming to cross the assurances the witches gave willingly), Hecate revives his spirits with a show of her power (which is now his). When Doctor Faustus is disconcerted by the action of his blood in signing the devil's compact, his familiar responds exactly as Hecate does to Macbeth's fear: Mephistopheles says, "I'll fetch him somewhat to delight his mind," and brings devils to dance in a pageant before him, while robing him in rich apparel. Faustus asks, "What means this show?"[41]

The diabolical machinery of *Macbeth* has an internal logic related to that of similar witch plays. Thus, whether the songs that appear both here and in Middleton's *The Witch* were written by Middleton or not, first written for *Macbeth* or not, the play as performed by Shakespeare's troupe makes dramatic sense. The Folio text is closer to Shakespeare's work than a putative 1606 text constructed out of modern editors' tastes by simply excising what they do not like in the Folio.

So far I have been looking only at the internal coherence of the diabolic order in *Macbeth,* as compared with the hellish regimen in the other Gunpowder plays (and in other witch plays). In all of them, traffic with the devil mounts a threat to good government and involves the traffickers with a devilish *community* of lower and higher spirits. It is necessary, now, to look more closely at Macbeth's relation to the witches' world.

three

Male Witch

the night's predominance

The preceding chapter examined *where* the witches meet—at a battlefield. This chapter will ask *when* and *how* the witches meet—by day, and in flight. As the witches fly *off* in different directions (hovering in fog), so they flew *on* from different directions.

Multiple entries were difficult on Shakespeare's stage. Modern actors can emerge from backdrops, or be caught hurrying in when the curtain or the stage lights go up. But David Bradley has shown how rare in Shakespeare's time was the simultaneous entry of characters from more than two directions (the two stage doors).[1] The problem is solved if the witches meet on an upper level with several entries, like that used in the Monument scenes of the contemporary play, *Antony and Cleopatra*. The text proves these witches are pausing (hovering) in mid-flight, above the battle.

More puzzling, however, is the fact that they meet by day, before the battle's "hurlyburly" is ended. Witches could not, ordinarily, fly by day. They needed the "thick" humors of night to bear them up.

The devil, according to King James, lifts them, then, by the same means he uses to make them invisible: he can "thicken and obscure so the air that is next about them by contracting it strait together."[2] Yet even in the day, a storm can "strangle" the sun, can "unnaturally" produce the "filthy air" that Richard Burton called the devil's vehicle: "Storms foster madness, and devils ride in their combustible air . . . The devil many times takes his opportunity in such storms, and when the humors by the air be stirred, he goes in with them [and] exagitates our spirit . . . ."[3] Macbeth himself recognizes this when he says: "Infected be the air *whereon they ride*" (4.1.138). Hecate, about to fly off, says her familiar spirit "sits in a foggy cloud" (3.5.35) that will bear up their car. In *The Devil's Charter* (lines 1943–45), Barnes writes that the devil

> rides triumphing in a chariot
> On misty-black clouds, mix'd with quenchless fire,
> Through uncouth corners in dark paths of death.

The witches put an *instrumental* stress on the preposition in the prologue's last line: "Hover *through* the fog and filthy air."[4]

The storm that batters the play's opening scene is, therefore, not just a matter of stage atmospherics or dramatic imagery. It is the necessary condition of the witches' abnormal activity by day. Lancelot Andrewes, in his first Gunpowder sermon, noted that devils work in "foul" days more than in "fair" ones:

> As for black and dismal days, days of sorrow and sad accident, they are, and may be counted (saith Job) for no-days—nights, rather, as having the shadow of death upon them. Or, *if* days, such as his [Job's] were, which Satan [rather] had marred than which God had made.[5]

Andrewes is describing the dark day of the Gunpowder Plot. Darkness is not just a mood-setter for Shakespeare's characters. It is a *constitutive* element of diabolic activity. Some ingredients of witches' spells not only have to be *used* at night, but *gathered* by night, in order to have full potency. This explains the witches' busy night activity at 3.5, to prepare for meeting Macbeth on the next morning. For some items, not even night is a sufficient environment—it must be a starless night, or (even better) a night in which the moon is erased by an eclipse. In this play, one witch proudly produces "slips of yew / sliver'd in the moon's eclipse" (4.1.28).[6] When the Duchess of Gloucester wants to start conjuring immediately, she is told that the right time for raising spirits must be chosen:

> Wizards know their times—
> Deep night, dark night, the silent of the night. . . .
> That time best fits the work we have in hand.[7]

Middleton's witch instructs another Duchess to "stay but time's perfection," which will be "owlet-time," when the night owls cry (5.2.38). Doctor Faustus is learned enough to know that he cannot conjure until black humors take over the sky:

> Now that the gloomy shadow of the night,
> Longing to view Orion's drizzling look,
> Leaps from th' Antarctic world unto the sky
> And dims the welkin with her pitchy breath,
> Faustus, begin thine invocations. . . .[8]

As the Christian liturgy has feasts of light, the devil's rites need darkness for them to be efficacious. That shows how wrong are the editors or directors who portray the witches, meeting Macbeth "ere the set of sun," as gathered in their covens or at their "sabbath" site. Their regular activity comes *after* sunset, and mainly at the midnight hour. Macbeth understands that. When he goes to meet them in their own lair, he calls them "Secret, black and midnight hags" (4.1.48) even though he is meeting them by day. They are *black hags* just as their leader is, in Macbeth's earlier words, "black Hecat" (3.2.41)— black by office and function. They are "midnight hags" as the poisons in *Hamlet* come from "midnight weeds . . . With Hecat's ban thrice blasted, thrice infected" (3.2.257–58).

Macbeth is attuned to these forces, to what he calls "night's black agents" (3.2.53), by his own "black desires" (1.4.51). Night is an *agent* as well as a setting in this play. It is an enabling force for evil, an ingredient in evil acts. Night collaborates with crime, as we can see by comparing Lady Macbeth's words with those of King James in *Daemonologie:*

> Come, *thick* Night,
> And pall thee in the dunnest smoke of Hell,
> That my keen knife *see* not the wound it makes,
> Nor heaven peep through the blanket of the dark
> To cry, "Hold! Hold!"

The devil can *"thicken* and obscure so the air . . . that the beams of any other man's eye cannot pierce through the same to *see* them."[9]

As Macbeth moves toward his chosen encounter with the witches, his invocations of darkness become more and more explicit— approximating, increasingly, the witches' technical forms of invocation. We can trace these steps toward his necromantic act as stages in a descent toward hell. There are three main steps down.

The first occurs as soon as the play's first night descends. Shakespeare carefully marked the hours in *Macbeth*'s early scenes.[10] The witches meet while the battle is still raging, and they have time to go on distant errands and return for their late-afternoon encounter with Macbeth. That encounter is long enough before "the set of sun" for Macbeth to remark on the foul lack of daylight in the day. Messengers arrive with news of Macbeth's promotion as night is coming on, and Macbeth receives his new title from the king in the early evening. Deep night has arrived by the time Macbeth looks up and asks for the stars to be blotted out (1.4.50–53).

> Stars, hide your fires!
> Let not light see my black and deep desires.
> The eye wink at the hand—yet let that be
> Which the eye fears (when it is done) to see.

Macbeth is calling for the kind of night witches exploit—when stars are "blinded" (Marston), the moon eclipsed, no light available to "profane" in reverse the perfect black. This darkness is so dissociative of acts from knowledge that Macbeth wants his own eye not to see his own hand. Lady Macbeth will shortly go beyond him and want even her *knife* not to "see" what it does. This inner division of one's acts from one's responsibility for them is what the two murderers seek. Macbeth will find night empowering as he becomes more and more a creature of the darkness.

The murder of Duncan takes place at the end of another day we watch descend. The king arrives when the castle eaves and their deceptively domestic birds are still visible. But after Macbeth is coaxed back into his resolve by his wife, it is already night—and another starless one, as Banquo notes at 2.1.5: "*Their* candles are all out." Macbeth is doing something more than "psyching himself" up to murder when he equates his act with the rites of witches in the night. This is his second invocation of darkness (2.1.49–56):

> Now, o'er the one half-world,
> Nature seems dead, and wicked dreams abuse
> The curtain'd sleep. Witchcraft celebrates
> Pale Hecat's off'rings, and wither'd Murder,
> Alarumed by his sentinel, the wolf
> (Whose howl's his watch), thus with his stealthy pace,
> With Tarquin's ravishing sights towards *his* design,
> Moves like a ghost.[11]

This passage is laden with witch language. To ab-use nature is the work of the devil, which makes *abuse* a technical term of craft.[12] Hamlet fears that the devil "abuses me to damn me" (2.2.603). Othello, called a male witch by Brabantio, is put on trial as an "abuser of the world" (1.2.78).[13] Macbeth himself will later be under his own spell, his "strange-and-self-abuse" (3.4.141).[14]

Murder is seen as a witch attended by his familiar, the wolf, whose cry is like that of Graymalkin in the earlier witch scenes. It is the right time for Hecate's offerings, and murder would lose some of its power if horror were taken from the time (2.1.56–60).

> Thou sure-and-firm-set Earth,
> Hear not my steps which way they walk, for fear
> The very stones prate of my whereabout
> And take the present horror from the time
> Which now suits with it.[15]

Fitting the time to the deed is the work of what Middleton's witch called (at 5.2.12) the "perfection of the time." To prevent God's natural works from witnessing dark events, the witch draws her magic circle. That creates "exempt space," outside God's providence. Long before Macbeth goes to the conjuring scene, where an actual circle is drawn, he is pulling a wizard's barrier around himself, to cut himself off from sky and earth and God.

Night descends a third time, its coming carefully described, when Banquo is to be murdered. Banquo has said he will be back for the feast (at seven) if he does not become "a borrower of the night / For a dark hour or twain" (3.1.26–27). Macbeth says "adieu / Till you return at night" (3.1.34–35), and instructs the murderers that their deed "must be done tonight" (130). Fleance, too, must "embrace the fate / Of that dark hour" (136–37).

Just before he goes in to the feast, Macbeth speaks his third invocation of the night. He precedes it with another descriptive reference to Hecate (3.2.40–44).

> Ere the bat hath flown
> His cloister'd flight, ere to black Hecat's summons
> The shard-borne beetle, with his drowsy hums,
> Hath rung night's yawning peal, there shall be done
> A deed of dreadful note.

All this will happen before midnight, Hecate's hour; the witches' familiar spirits are already bustling about. The beetle is a familiar, like the cricket; the bat is a familiar almost as common as the cat.[16]

In the formal invocation spoken after Macbeth tells Lady Macbeth to be innocent of such occult-and-guilty knowledge, he addresses Night directly for the first time (3.2.46–52):

> Come, seeling Night,
> Scarf up the tender eye of pitiful day
> And, with thy bloody-and-invisible hand,

> Cancel and tear to pieces that Great Bond
> Which keeps me pale. Light thickens, and the crow
> Makes wing t' th' rooky wood.
> Good things of day begin to droop and drowse
> Whiles Night's black agents to their preys do rouse.

On no passage is there less agreement, among editors and commentators, than on the Folio's "great Bond" in line 49. It has been called Banquo's life (Steevens), the witches' pronouncement (Moberly), love (Foakes), guilt (Libby), the moral law (Hunter), the cosmos (Brooke). Keightley emended to "band," and Muir prefers that (Trevor Nunn adopted the reading in his production).

Where guesses range so wide, we must stick to the narrowing conditions of the bond's description. It is a document of some sort that can be figuratively torn up and canceled. And it keeps Macbeth pale. "Binding" is a common description of witches' action; but this bond hinders Macbeth's murderous career. It is a bond *on the other side*, one competing with evil's power to hold one committed to an evil course. What competes with the diabolic engagement? The answer is given by the legal discussion of witchcraft in William West's *Symbolaeographie* (1594): "These wicked persons, by oath or writing (written with their own blood) having betaken themselves to the devil, have forsaken God and *broken their covenant made in baptism*. . . ."[17] This is the greatest bond, the new covenant in baptism that replaced for Christians the old covenant in circumcision.[18] To renounce this is the great renunciation, as Iago knows when he says that Desdemona could get Othello to do anything, "were't to renounce his baptism" (2.3.334).

The devil's compact is a parody and cancelation of the rites of baptism. The shedding of blood to form the devil's mark is a mock circumcision; the pact is an anti-baptism certificate. In the baptismal formula, one renounces the devil and all his works. In the devil's pact, one renounces that renunciation.[19] This bond includes one in the Christian community which Pauline scripture calls the saved soul's bond [*syndesmos,* the Vulgate's *vinculum*] of peace (Ephesians 4.3) and bond of perfectness (Colossians 3.4). There is even a reference to the white baptismal gown in Macbeth's lament that the Great Bond still keeps him pale. Some editors have suggested that the terminology of bond makes for a pun at "seeling (and *sealing*) Night." Theologians regularly saw a reference to baptism in the Pauline expression "sealed with the Spirit" (Ephesians 1.13; II Corinthians 1.22). Night, as the *canceler* of baptism, seals *its* followers with the devil's mark (see Chapter Four below).

When "light thickens," the humors of darkness enable black forces to work. The devil's power is loosed at two moments in the gospels— when Jesus is in agony the night before his crucifixion ("This is your hour, and the power of darkness," Luke 22.53) and when the sky is darkened, turning day to night, at Jesus' death ("There was darkness over the whole land," Mark 15.33). These passages gave the theological warrant for finding diabolic powers roaming free at night, or on unnaturally darkened days.

Even those of more skeptical bent found something efficacious in blackness itself. Samuel Harsnett, dismissing witch delusions, thought they arose, nonetheless, out of black humors "because from this black and sooty blood, gloomy fuliginous spirits do fume into the brain."[20] Many, like Robert Burton, combined physiology and theology to say that black humors are nature's vulnerable point for the entry of real devils.[21] However one explains the connection, night and the devil go together. That is what Macbeth is talking about when he says that

Night's black agents use the darkness to move against their prey. This is not a reference to predators in the animal kingdom. It is closer to Banquo's description (1.3.124–26) of "the instruments of darkness" that "betray us in deepest consequence" (i.e., into damnation). Macbeth is about to traffic openly with those instruments of darkness.

The power of night in this play is seen from the fact that we watch three nights come over the action, and three days *fail* to come. The nights that descend, in carefully described stages, are: the one that closes the opening day of battle, the one in which Duncan is killed, and the one in which Banquo is killed. The days that *fail* to come are the foul day of the battle itself, and each day that follows on the murders. After Duncan's assassination, Ross notes that the sun refuses to shine (2.4.5–10):

> Thou seest the heavens, as troubled with man's act,
> Threatens his bloody stage. By th' clock tis day,
> And yet dark night strangles the traveling lamp.
> Is't night's predominance or the day's shame
> That darkness does the face of earth entomb
> When living light should kiss it?

Night's *predominance* is an astrological term, suggesting a cosmic "takeover" by night, an encroachment on the proper domain of day.[22]

The third day obscured and turned to night is that which follows on Banquo's death. We have already learned that Macbeth means to seek out the witches on this day (3.4.131–32):

> I will tomorrow—
> And betimes I will—to the Weyard Sisters.

Macbeth speaks after the banquet, when night verges toward day. Macbeth asks "What is the night?" His Lady responds (3.4.126):

Almost at odds with morning which is which.

In the next scene. Hecate is urging on her witches to complete their preparations by night—she herself must get a poison drop as it falls from the moon, so they can meet Macbeth in the morning: "Great business must be wrought ere noon" (3.5.22).[23] She flies off in a "foggy cloud" (3.5.35), and Macbeth appears at the witches' lair to stage directions of thunder. This is another unnaturally dark day— the boundaries between light and darkness are being erased in Scotland.

When Macbeth sets out consciously to "know, by the worst means, the worst" from the witches (3.4.133–34), he is exposing himself to the same laws that made Sir Edward Kelley (in real life) and the Duchess of Gloucester (in Shakespeare's play) guilty of necromancy—i.e., of witchcraft. He appeals to the witches in the name of their art, of their dark knowledge, no matter what its source (4.1.50–51):

> I conjure you, by that which you profess,
> How e'er you come to know it, answer me.[24]

He has addressed them in terms of their office:

> How now you secret, black, and midnight hags.

This is the way Ovid's Medea begins to conjure Night: "Oh, Night, you secret-keeper!"

> *Nox, ait, arcanis fidissima . . .*[25]

This is not an accidental resemblance. The model for Macbeth's conjuring speech is the classical speech of Medea best known to Shakespeare in Ovid's and in Seneca's versions of it.[26] It has long been recognized that Shakespeare based Prospero's description of his magic on Ovid's Medea; but Macbeth's speech is just as close to that model.

Macbeth asks for knowledge on the basis of witches' power to wrest, from an unwilling nature, compelled submission. To emphasize this he lists the classical *adynata* (feats beyond natural causation) that make up the canonical list of witches' boasts. Medea, like other classical witches, says she can draw down the moon, move crops around, invert the seasons, reverse river currents, turn everything topsyturvy.[27] Here is Macbeth's use of that classical witch-catalogue (4.1.52–59):

> Though you untie the winds and let them fight
> Against the churches, though the yesty waves
> Confound and swallow navigation up,
> Though bladed corn be lodg'd and trees blown down,
> Though castles topple on their warders' heads,
> Though palaces and pyramids do slope
> Their heads to their foundations, though the treasure
> Of nature's germens tumble all together
> Even till destruction sicken, answer me . . .

This kind of speech, often imitated from the classical sources, is almost always put into the mouth of a witch or the queen of witches. Ben Jonson, for instance, has Hecate say:

> When we have set the elements at wars,
> Made midnight see the sun, and day the stars;
> When the winged lightning in its course hath stay'd,
> And swiftest rivers have run back, afraid
> To see the corn remove, the graves to range

> While places alter and the seas do change;
> When the pale moon, at the first voice, down fell
> Poison'd, and durst not stay the second spell . . .[28]

Although Macbeth's *adynata*, like Jonson's, are classical, there is one Christian touch in Shakespeare that makes its "modern" witchcraft more explicit. Macbeth not only says he will set the winds at war—a typical feature of witch-boasting—but that he will make them war *against the churches*.[29] That is an extra touch of malice that Doctor Faustus shares with Macbeth. Faustus says that he will "make my spirit pull his churches down" (A2.3.98).

The classical basis of Macbeth's witchcraft makes it especially odd for people to object to Hecate's appearance in this scene as clashing with the witch-spells on the heath. Macbeth sees no contradiction in using classical concepts to address the hags. In fact, "folk" and classical motifs mix in all the dramatic treatments of witches in 1606—for a very good reason: Those who believed in witchcraft thought it was a permanent feature in history, ever since its master tempted Eve in Eden.

Besides, some of the touches in the play's treatment of Hecate come from the same sources as Macbeth's own speech. Hecate is said to "look angerly" when she first appears (3.5.1), and at Seneca, *Medea*, 751, she is *fronte non una minax* "frowning triple menace." (Studley's translation says she "knit'st more threat'ning brows than one.") Hecate says she will catch "a vap'rous drop profound" as it falls from the moon to the earth (3.5.23–25)—and Ovid's Medea, making a potion under Hecate's guidance, uses "frost vapor gathered by the full moon" (*exceptas luna pernocte pruinas*, 268).[30] This does not so much indicate a direct source for Shakespeare's line as a general concordance of atmosphere between Macbeth's speech (whose genuineness no one has challenged) and the Hecate scenes. Macbeth expected to meet Hecate as well as the witches. He has invoked her in the past, and he is asking the witches to stretch all their powers. Tumbling the universe's elements to confusion is a task for their superiors, and he knows it as he moves within their orb.

The "double toil" the witches have prepared is a *net* to trammel Macbeth, not a *labor* on their part. Antony is caught in Cleopatra's "strong toil of grace." Decius will catch Caesar with flattery, as easily as one might "catch lions with toils."[31]

Brought to the conjuring scene—always considered a place of peril, since controlled devils can go *out* of control—Macbeth must submit to the customary discipline. He is enjoined to silence (4.1.70):

Hear his speech but say thou nought.

The command is repeated between apparitions (4.1.89):

Listen, but speak not to 't.

This is part of the ritual in most stage necromancies. The Duchess of Gloucester is told to sit quietly during the conjuring (*II Henry VI* 1.4.15–22). When the Pope conjures in *The Devil's Charter*, the devils he has raised enjoin him twice (lines 1935, 1950)

Keep a firm station, stir not for thy life.

Faustus, when he conjures for others, admonishes them: "Be silent, then, for danger is in words" (A5.1.25). The ignorant initiate can jumble the magic formulas by interjecting non-ritual words.

In all these scenes, occult learning is shown off by the actors—so detailed in the case of Marlowe's play that there was more than one story of people in the audience showing fright that the devil would actually answer such a proper summons.[32]

The basic art of conjuring involved creation of the charmed circle. Sometimes the conjurers must stay clear of the circle, the dangerous arena of the devil. Sometimes they must stay inside it, protected from God's law so long as they inhabit "allowed space" (Frontispiece). Faustus is learned in his alignment of the circle with the streams of noxious influences on the particular night. He wheels the universe backward, as it were, just as his spells reverse holy names and phrases (A1.3.8–13):

> Within this circle is Jehovah's name
> Forward and backward anagrammatis'd—
> The breviated names of holy saints,
> Figures of ev'ry adjunct to the heaven,
> And characters of signs and erring stars—
> By which the spirits are enforc'd to rise.[33]

After this learned bit of conjuring raises Mephistopheles, that spirit teaches Faustus more advanced circle technique (A2.2.163–65):

> The iterating of *these* lines brings gold;
> The framing of *this* circle on the ground
> Brings whirlwinds, tempests, thunder and lightning;
> Pronounce *this* thrice devoutly to thyself . . .

The conjuring scene in Barnes's play (performed, remember, by Shakespeare's troupe) is even more complex than those in Faustus. First an assistant creates a "fumigation"—incensing with coals. After that, *"Alexander fashioneth out his circle; then taketh his rod . . . standing without the circle he waveth his rod to the East."*[34] He has already done his astrological calculations, on which the proper drawing of the circle is based.

Alexander cometh upon the stage out of his study, with a book in his hand.

I perfectly perceive
By this ascension of Arctophilax
What time of night it is . . .[35]

Then the Pope recites Latin formulas, giving the secret names of devils—an act which corresponds, in *Macbeth* as we have it, to Hecate's call to her different spirits (4.1.44–48, Brooke edition).

Where is the circle in *Macbeth*'s conjuring scene? The witches do not draw mystic marks on the ground. The cauldron itself is too small for the kind of circles seen in *Doctor Faustus* or *The Devil's Charter*. The witches trace the circle with their dance—they "charm" the precinct they define as they move all around it. "Round about the cauldron go," they sing as they make triple repetitions of triple formulae, calling on their familiars ("Thrice the brindled cat hath mewed"). They had done a quick "charming" in their meeting on the heath (1.3.32–37):

WITCHES:	The Weyard Sisters, hand in hand, Posters of the sea and land, Thus do go about, about.
FIRST WITCH:	Thrice to thine.
SECOND WITCH:	And thrice to mine.
THIRD WITCH:	And thrice again, to make up nine.
WITCHES:	Peace, the charm's wound up.

It seems likely that Macbeth, when he enters, steps unconsciously into the charmed circle, and the witches circle him with their triple "Hails," cutting him off from Banquo. After Macbeth steps out to pursue the witches, and then to greet Ross, he returns to the circle and is again cut off from his fellows for the soliloquy that fills him with "horrible imaginings," making his heart race and his hair bristle. He is on dangerous ground.

We expect something more complex and mystical in the conjuring scene itself—and this is another reason to accept Hecate's activity. The first three witches may have performed a more complete ritual in the 1606 version, but in the text as we have it they simply circle the cauldron while they throw in vile ingredients. They do not have to do more. Hecate marshals her singers and dancers "in a ring," calling on many spirits as a vast circle is created, traced by the six witches' combined forces (4.1.49–50, Brooke).

> Round, around, around, about, about,
> All ill come running in, all good keep out.

This, too, is a circle one stands *inside*, *with* the forces of evil. So when the witch says (4.1.45),

> Something wicked this way comes,

Macbeth is drawn into the circle where all ills congregate.

The witches would clearly dance as the magician traces his circle, doing everything *backward*, from the cursed and cursing left hand, not the divine right hand. Ben Jonson described this kind of dancing in his stage directions for the witches in *The Masque of Queens*:

> At which, with a strange and sudden music, they fall into a magical and pre-pos-terous [stationing posterior in front] change and ges-

ticulation, but most applying to their property [proper office] who, at
their meetings, do all things contrary to the custom of men, dancing
back to back and hip to hip, their hands joined, and *making their circles backward to the left hand. . . .*[36]

The second team of witches, tracing a larger circle around the one
made by the first three (as they put things in the cauldron) literally
creates a "double toil" on the ground—and Macbeth enters into this
network of charmed boundaries. The extra witches seem to withdraw
as Macbeth faces the apparitions—the stage has to be partly cleared for
the later procession of kings. Hecate all the while would preside over
the scene from a gallery, or upper level, the place where Lucifer and
Beelzebub appeared for their silent scenes in *Doctor Faustus.*

Macbeth must stand close to the cauldron—while being warned
against interference with the rite—as the witches circle him (to the
left) for their three introductions of the visions. Dramatically, it
would be most effective if he stands facing the audience, on the other
side of the cauldron, since—by contrast—he must turn to see the
procession of kings that passes *outside the circle* in which he is pent.

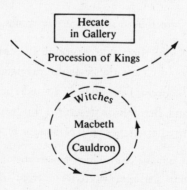

Macbeth is integrated into the witch proceeding, but kept clear of the royal legitimacy.

What is the significance of the three visions? The armed head that warns against Macduff is a stage property Greene made popular with Friar Bacon's speaking "Brass Head." It is armed because Macbeth is a soldier who must brace himself for Macduff's military attack. In a 1916 American production of the play, Macduff wears the speaking head's helmet when he kills Macbeth in the last act.[37] The head, without Macbeth's realizing it, *introduces* the next vision, the bloody babe rising from the cauldron (which speaks with a treble voice). It is a vision of a child "torn from the womb" by Caesarean section, though Macbeth would interpret it as the death of any baby "born of woman" who might grow up to threaten him—it is a hint (in his own eyes) to be acted on when he turns Macduff's son into a "bloody babe." The last vision, a kingly child with a tree of fertility as his sceptre, makes the prophecy that should alert Macbeth to the emptiness of the assurances being given him. Birnam Wood can be moved, since *silvas moveo* is a standard witch's boast—he had even suggested this in his own list of *adynata* ("trees blown down"). But the crown on the child diverts Macbeth into the question that produces the kingly procession.

Macbeth turns, but stays inside the circle, as Banquo reappears, looking just as he had at the banquet, still "blood-balter'd" (4.1.123)— making a vivid connection with the "bloody child," uniting the two kinds of vision. The entry of the bloodied corpse should jolt us, here, since it repeats the way Banquo appeared behind Macbeth's back in the banquet scene.[38] Banquo leads on the kings and, circling backstage, reappears to finish the procession—exactly as the devil escorts the murdered and murdering pairs in the conjured procession of *The Devil's Charter.*

Macbeth goes forth from the conjuring scene with a new sense of power. That is misunderstood by some who ask why Macbeth repeatedly curses the witches. When the sisters try to deny his requests, saying, "Seek to know no more" (4.1.103), he says: "Deny me this / And an eternal curse fall on you!" Then, after he has seen the infernal procession, he says (4.1.133–34):

> Let this pernicious hour
> Stand aye accursed in the calendar!

After Lennox joins him, he says of the witches (4.1.138–39):

> Infected be the air whereon they ride,
> And damn'd all those that trust them!

That sounds, to our ears, as if Macbeth had failed of his purpose and regretted coming. But this cannot be the case. He puts out of his mind the bad news (lulled by Hecate's "cheering" song) and retains a confidence in his invulnerability, one based on the "promise" that no one born of woman will kill him and that Birnam Wood must move before he dies.

For a contractor with the devil to curse the intermediaries is common—not all requests can be granted.[39] When this happens, or other misgivings arise at the perilous course conjurers are embarked on, a Doctor Faustus can say "Curse thee, wicked Mephistopheles!" (A2.3.2). This explains Macbeth's first two curses. His last one is said to mislead Lennox, to pretend he has not engaged in criminal dealings with the witches. This is one of those cases where an unconscious irony makes Macbeth's lies come out as truths.⁴⁰ He shall find, indeed, that "damn'd [be] all those that trust them."

Macbeth *does* trust the witches. He has pawned his soul to get the precious knowledge they seem to have given him. He is now a man apart, a dizzying fact that incites fearful glee in Faustus and other witches. The dire consequences of conjuring are underlined in all the witch plays. Merely to summon occult knowledge is to step across a boundary, to negotiate with hell. Mephistopheles explains to Faustus the deeper meaning of his act (A1.3.46–52):

FAUSTUS: Did not my conjuring speeches raise thee? Speak.

MEPHISTOPHELES: That was the cause, but yet *per accidens.*
                 For when we hear one rack the name of God,
                 Abjure the Scriptures and his Savior Christ,
                 We fly in hope to get his glorious soul.
                 Nor will we come unless he use such means
                 Whereby he is in danger to be damn'd.

This is the doctrine of the philosophical dog-familiar in *The Witch of Edmonton* (5.1.128–30):

Thou never art so distant
From an evil spirit but that thy oaths,
Curses, and blasphemies pull him to thine elbow.

That is the dreadful reality behind all the theatrical effects of the necromancy scene—which is, as Peter Stallybrass says, "the emblematic center of the play."⁴¹ Macbeth is a different man after he has undergone this rite.

Some modern productions try to suggest the encounter with hell by having Macbeth enter the conjuring scene by a long stage descent.

John Wilkes Booth even anticipated his leap from box to stage after killing President Lincoln when, playing Macbeth in 1860, he leaped twelve feet from a ledge to get down to the witches' cauldron.[42] But the witches in their own home were menacing enough to Shakespeare's audience. That audience knew the price of power obtained through diabolic intercession. So did Charles Macready, who accomplished on the Victorian stage what Olivier did in 1955, growing monstrously to a giant end out of the mad certitudes drawn from the cauldron. Macready, too, was greatest in the last act, and he deepened his sense of the damned soul's defiance by reading *Paradise Lost* while performing *Macbeth*.[43] Some have called Lady Macbeth the "fourth witch" in the play, or the "real witch." But she never commits the formal crime of conjuring and necromancy. Macbeth, like other acknowledged witches in Shakespeare, does.[44] In fact, he is one of the great male witches of drama—like Marlowe's Doctor Faustus, like Barnes's Pope Alexander, or like the Faustian Jesuit Campeius (Campion) in Dekker's *The Whore of Babylon*.[45]

Some, in thrall to the typical image of the witch as woman, would prefer to say that Macbeth engages in sorcery, rather than that he is himself a sorcerer. But necromancy is the *crime* of witchcraft, and he commits it. Margery Jourdain conjured for the Duchess of Gloucester, but the Duchess underwent the witch's punishment (see Chapter Four). That Shakespeare presents Macbeth as a witch is apparent from the Medea-speech he gives to him. That language is used, elsewhere, *only* by witches (including the "white witch," Prospero). Harsnett called the Jesuits "devil-conjurors"—i.e., witches—and the Jesuit connection is strong in this play.[46]

four

Lady Macbeth

damned spot

Though Lady Macbeth's is not a huge part—she speaks only a third of the lines that Cleopatra does, and under half of Portia's in *The Merchant of Venice*—two towering (but very different) theatrical reputations were built largely on performances as Lady Macbeth: Sarah Siddons's in the eighteenth century and Ellen Terry's in the nineteenth.[1] Siddons was the lofty terrorizer of her husband, and Terry the pre-Raphaelite spectre who dooms him with her beauty. No actor of modern times—since, that is, the inception of the "curse" on the play—has won such general recognition for excelling in this part, though presumably even Siddons and Terry may have fallen short of the first Lady Macbeth, John Rice.

Shakespeare's greatest parts for women naturally cluster at periods when the playwright had an outstanding boy actor, and the lead boy in 1606–07 had three choice parts in a row—Shakespeare's Lady Macbeth and Cleopatra, as well as Barnes's Lucretia in *The Devil's Charter*.[2] (The actor may, in fact, have had a fourth great role if the view that a boy played the Fool in *Lear* is right.)[3]

Who was that boy? All the evidence points to John Rice. He was singled out, along with the lead adult actor Richard Burbage, to appear before the King in an ambitious program financed by the Merchant Taylors of London in the summer of 1607.[4] Rice was elaborately costumed for the occasion.[5] Though his speech—specially composed by Ben Jonson—only ran to twelve lines, brilliant delivery was important to the spectacle. Rice's master, John Heminges, was paid forty shillings "for his direction of his boy that made the speech to His Majesty," while the boy got five shillings.[6]

Burbage and Rice obviously made a winning pair, since they appeared together in at least one other special performance, three years later—this one to welcome Prince Henry's arrival in London. Anthony Munday wrote the lines performed by Burbage as Amphion, and Rice as Corinea.[7] Rice, who went on to a distinguished acting career as an adult before becoming a clergyman, obviously had grace, good looks, and sweet diction in 1607, when Shakespeare wrote for him the demanding part of Cleopatra, performed at court in the Christmas season of 1606–07.[8]

That was an amazing season. It is known that the King's Men acted *Lear* on the day after Christmas and *The Devil's Charter* on Candlemas (February 2). There is growing belief that *Macbeth* and *Antony and Cleopatra* were also acted in the season—a break-out time after the long closing of the public theatres by the plague.[9] A remarkable feature of all of these plays is their fascination with witchcraft. *Antony* constantly refers to Cleopatra as having witch-like powers.[10] Lucretia in *The Devil's Charter* is not only the daughter of the conjuring male witch, Pope Alexander; she independently calls on hell's assistance for murdering her husband (lines 601–5):

You grisly daughter of grim Erebus,
Which spit out venom from your vip'rous hairs,
Infuse a threefold vigor in these arms,
Immarble more my strong indurate heart,
To consummate the plot of my revenge.

Compare Rice's other great role, as Cleopatra (5.2.238–40):

I have nothing
Of woman in me. Now, from head to foot
I am marble-constant.

And compare *those* lines with Lady Macbeth's (1.5.42–43):

And fill me, from the crown to th' toe, topful
Of direst cruelty.

All these heroines ask to be made inhumanly "indurate" for their evil tasks.

Make thick my blood,
Stop up th' access and passage to remorse,
That no compunctious visitings of nature
Shake my fell purpose.[11]

This clustering of Rice's roles with a witch-like aspect (Lucretia Borgia, Cleopatra, Lady Macbeth) would seem to support those who consider Lady Macbeth the "fourth witch" of the play.[12] Directors have emphasized her evil nature by associating her with the witches visually, or even by having her double the role of Hecate.[13] It is true that she invokes Night and "murth'ring ministers" (demons)—just as her husband invokes Night and Hecate. Her evil ministers are clearly the fallen counterparts of angelic "ministers of grace" called on by Hamlet (1.4.39).[14]

In fact, Lady Macbeth's grand invocation at 1.5.40–54 is full of "witch talk." She orders the evil spirits to "unsex me here"—and witches were famously unsexed, a fact emphasized in *Macbeth*'s three witches, played by men. Banquo remarks on their beards at 1.3.45–47, as Hamlet does on the boy actor who had grown up to adult (bearded) parts at *Hamlet* 2.2.423. The witches' sexual traffic with devils was considered one consequence of their loss of sexual attractiveness for men. Lady Macbeth plays with the idea of that sexual traffic with devils when she calls the demons: "Come to my woman's breasts / And take my milk for gall."[15] Witches nursed their familiars from their "marks," considered as teats for diabolic nourishment. Since the marks were often near witches' "privy parts," the nursing could be a kind of foreplay preceding intercourse.[16] La Pucelle calls on her familiars with a reminder how "I was wont to feed you with my blood" (*I Henry VI* 5.3.14).[17] Joan's familiars, when they abandon her, refuse the offered teats, unlike other familiars, who feed onstage. In *The Witches of Edmonton*, the dog-familiar is seen sucking a mark on Mother Sawyer's arm (2.1.147), and another character describes the way he will "creep under an old witch's coats and suck like a great puppy" (5.1.173–74). Mother Sawyer says her mark has dried up, and asks the dog (4.1.157–60) to

> Stand on thy hind legs—up, kiss me, my Tommy,
> And rub some wrinkles on my brow
> By making my old ribs shrug for joy
> Of thy fine tricks. What hast thou done? Let's tickle!

Hecate, who is a witch not a goddess in Middleton's *The Witch*, calls to her familiar, the actor in a cat costume (3.3.49–50):

> Here's one come down to fetch his dues—
> A kiss, a coll [hug], a sip of blood.

She has had sex with this familiar (1.2.96–97). In *The Late Lancashire Witches*, a witch is asked, "Hath thy puggy [little Puck] yet suck'd upon thy pretty duggy?" (line 2017).

The image of witches giving suck to animals was deep in the lore of Shakespeare's time.[18] Some resist having Lady Macbeth use this image; but we should remember that John Rice's other part at the time, Cleopatra, involved a witch-like comparison of the serpent's bite to an animal familiar's sucking (*Antony* 5.2.309–10):

> Dost thou not see my baby at my breast
> That sucks the nurse asleep?

Even before her cry to the evil spirits, Lady Macbeth was associated with an animal familiar. Hearing a caw from offstage, she says: "The raven himself is hoarse / That croaks the fatal enterance of Duncan / Under my battlements" (1.5.38–40).[19] His entry is fatal, as Hecate works "Unto a dismal and a fatal end" (3.5.21). The raven was a regular "familiar," and its loud cry from offstage had special theatrical effect. Indeed, one of the more spectacular sound effects of the Elizabethan stage was the massive cawing of ravens that fulfilled a prophecy and defeated an army in *Edward III*, a play to which Shakespeare may have contributed.[20]

It is likely that we have already heard the raven that crows over Lady Macbeth's castle. In the opening scene, when familiars summon their witches away, two spirits are named—Graymalkin, a cat, and Paddock, a toad. The third witch answers *her* spirit's call, "Anon." The raven's cry was too (yes) *familiar* to make identification necessary.

At 4.1.3, the third witch's animal is addressed as Harpier, an apparent nickname based on Harpy. The raven was a harpy, a food-snatcher.[21] When carrion birds settled on corpses, popular fear and loathing depicted them as witches' familiars gathering body parts. The witch literature fostered that belief. In Ben Jonson's *The Sad Shepherd*, a raven waits as huntsmen corner a deer, and its witch is later seen in a chimney corner with a morsel the bird delivered to her.[22] In *The Masque of Queens*, Jonson translated a passage from Lucan, in which a witch waits for a raven to snatch flesh off a corpse and then takes it from the raven.[23] The raven is a particularly unclean bird, whose very presence acts as a curse on a house, as Othello notes (4.1.20–22):

> It comes o'er my memory
> As doth the raven o'er the' infectious house
> Boding to all.

Thersites, when he dreams of cursing, does so as a raven in his own mind: "I would croak like a raven, I would bode, I would bode" (*Troilus* 5.2.191). Caliban uses the raven when he curses (*Tempest* 1.2.321–33):

> As wicked dew as e'er my [witch] mother brush'd,
> With raven's feather, from unwholesome fen
> Drop on you both!

Thus, for Lady Macbeth to welcome the raven's portent puts her in accord with witches' thoughts, with the Hecate of Middleton's *The Witch* (5.2.40–42):

> Raven or screech-owl never fly by the door
> But they call in, I thank 'em. And they lose not by't—
> I give 'em barley soaked in infant's blood.

Lady Macbeth's castle is an "infectious house" with fatal gates to welcome Duncan.

In all these ways, Lady Macbeth certainly *tries* to become an intimate of evil, a communer with murdering ministers, fatal ravens, spirits who will give her suck. Does that make her a witch? Not in any technically legal or theological sense that King James (for instance) would have recognized. She does not enter into supernatural dealings with devils or their agents. There is no reciprocal activity of the sort Macbeth engages in at the necromancy. She is a witch of velleity and gestures, while he is one in fact. She forms no pact with the devil. Hecate does not appear to comfort *her.*

All these are important indicators of the way the part should be played. Lady Macbeth's relation to her husband resembles that of Barnes's Lucretia Borgia to her incestuous father. We see Pope Alexander strike his bargain with the devil, and pay for it; but Lucretia's invocation of evil spirits is mainly a way of steeling herself to kill her husband. In that sense, it works. Like Lady Macbeth she is a murderess. Macbeth will take calculated steps deeper and deeper into collaboration with hellish forces, but Lady Macbeth falters early—as Macbeth realizes. After the murder of Duncan, he no longer relies on her help. He is looking to more powerful auxiliaries. "Be inn'cent of the knowledge, dearest chuck . . ." (3.2.45) was said with a kind of bemused tone of farewell by Olivier to Vivien Leigh. She is not hardened for the voyage he is taking by that time.[24]

Olivier seemed to some critics to underplay his early scenes because he was carefully counting the cost of his crime. He weighs the pros and cons of Duncan's murder. He observes his own reactions, testing his pulse as he moves forward. His moves are less impulsive— and less shallow—than his wife's immediate enthusiasm for the crime. When she wavers, it is from collapse, not calculation. She cannot kill the king because he looks like her father. She nerves herself with drink, claiming that it steadies her: "That which hath made them drunk hath made me bold" (2.2.1). But the drink is wearing off after the murder. She faints in the discovery scene—a genuine faint, not some shrewd attempt to distract people from Macbeth's embarrassment. Some have said it is impossible for an actress to make it clear why she is fainting. But of Vivien Leigh's faint it was written: "Genuine? Feigned? No need to ask the question. Her collapse was as inevitable a result of the dramatic process as is the spark when two charged wires are brought together."[25]

The trouble with the majestic Sarah Siddons approach to Lady Macbeth is that it plunges the character too abruptly into collapse after her time of splendid power. The long absence of Lady Macbeth from the play makes the contrast less bridgeable. The Byam Shaw production of 1955 made the later Lady Macbeth shine through the bravado of the earlier one. When Macbeth launched into his own baroque description of the way he executed the grooms, Olivier experienced a strange power in his ability to describe as well as to do the act—he was finding himself oddly at home in his crime, horrified but also fascinated. He is becoming a connoisseur of the sensations of evil. But Lady Macbeth is stunned by his glib description of the murder. As he speaks, she reacts hypnotically, moving toward him over an abyss. "The two seemed drawn together by the compulsion of their common guilt to the center of the stage."[26] She cannot complete the passage over the chasm opening between them. She faints just as she is about to reach him.

The two are similarly divided in the banquet scene—Macbeth living inside his murder of Banquo, his wife kept outside, trying (ineffectually) to mediate between him and the external world. They are never seen together again—in fact, she is seen only one more time. What explains her long absence from the play? One naturally thinks, in a theater so dependent on doubling (especially where boys are concerned), that John Rice must be busy in another role.[27] We have already seen that some directors want the modern actress to double Hecate; but that was impossible for Shakespeare. "Poel's Rule" states that a character who exits at the close of one scene does not enter at the opening of the next.[28] It is even less feasible, in the fluid conditions of Jacobean performance, for an actor to leave *as one character* and come right back on *as another*. Besides, Hecate would need some form of gorgeous costume to suggest her supernatural status—more than could be thrown on for instant reappearance.

But there is another role Rice could have doubled—Macduff's wife. The power of this doubling was suggested in Trevor Nunn's staging of the play in the close arena of Stratford's small Other Place. All the actors sat around the charmed circle of the play's action, stepping on when their parts called for it, watching the action when it did not. There was great power in the presence of Lady Macbeth at the murder of Lady Macduff's son. The woman who said she would tear her own child from her nipple and dash it to the ground now saw something like that imagined scene made real. This helped explain her disintegration in the sleepwalking scene.[29] Modern cinema could accomplish the same thing by showing the queen's imagination of the infanticide when she first heard of it. Shakespeare accomplished it by having one actor play both the self-violative mother and the cruelly violated Lady Macduff.[30]

In the well-lit open condition of the theater in Shakespeare's time, audiences recognized a doubling actor in his new guise. In fact, their favorites were *meant* to be recognized—e.g., the comic actor Armin: the Porter's jokes were carried by a comic persona he had developed and made popular. The spectators would know he was also playing a witch. But they accepted the convention that a new costume created a new part—just as they accepted the convention that a boy was a woman. This made disguises "convincing" in a way that it is hard for modern audiences to accept. (It seems odd to us that Viola could be so readily taken as identical in appearance to Sebastian in *Twelfth Night.*)

But the piquancy of some doubling would strike an audience, even under those conditions. I shall be suggesting one such effect in the next chapter, when I speak of Armin as a witch and as the Porter in hell. Others have noticed the appropriateness of King Lear's two loyal but truth-telling attendants, his quiet daughter, and his "allowed" satirist, being played by the same boy.

A similar increase in dramatic power comes from our seeing Lady Macbeth again only after Rice has played the womanly anguish of Lady Macduff. The impact of the sleepwalking scene was undoubtedly increased by that interval. We, in effect, fill up the void created by Lady Macbeth's absence with a communal female suffering. The fact that Lady Macduff was innocent and Lady Macbeth guilty just increases the pathos of the queen's repentance—for that, in effect, is what the scene amounts to. The first indication of this is the brief stage direction in the Folio: *Enter Lady with a Taper.* The punishment of a penitent witch involved her parading her crime by holding a taper (the symbol of witches' rites, which used candles as Catholic masses did, liturgically). Shakespeare made the Duchess of Gloucester submit to this form of "pillorying" in *II Henry VI* 2.4.17ff. The stage direction is: *Enter the Duchess in a white Sheet, and a Taper burning in her hand*. She tells her husband she is "mailed up in shame" by this penitential garb. We know this was the legal form of shaming, either before execution or (in lesser offences) as a substitute for it. The *Chronicle of London* describes the event Shakespeare put into his play:

> Landed at the Temple Bridge out of her barge . . . [she] openly, barehead, with a kerchief on her head baring, she took a taper of wax of two pounds in her hand, and went so through Fleet Street, on her feet and hoodless, into Paul's, and there she offered up her taper at the high altar.[31]

The Duchess was a repentant witch—and so, in her own mind, is Lady Macbeth. The stage direction names the taper, a huge one in the Duchess's case (two pounds, the size of the taper was gauged by the seriousness of the crime). There is a suggestion of something out of the ordinary in the Doctor's question: "How came she by that light?" The woman has told us the queen threw on her nightgown, and the scene is usually played barefoot, like the Duchess's. The taper-barefoot-sheet cluster said, to Shakespeare's audience, "repentant sorceress."

And we have other indications of Lady Macbeth's sense of guilt. She never became a witch, like her husband; but she entertained witch fantasies, which have come back to haunt her. She acts like a witch when she tries to rub out or efface her "damn'd spot" (5.1.35). The bloody spot most feared by those suspected of witchcraft was the devil's mark left on them when they sealed their compact.[32] Marlowe made much of this bloody sign when he had Faustus's blood congeal at the horror of what he was doing (A2.1.61–72). When at last the mark is made, it becomes a damned spot indeed, forming the words "Fly, man!" (*Home fuge*). Spots were evidence of the devil's ownership, a brand, a seal that could not be disowned. People arrested for witchcraft tried to cut or rub off any moles or blemishes that could be used against them. A Staffordshire investigator found that one Alice Gooderidge had "upon her belly a hole, of the bigness of two pence, fresh and bloody, as though some great wart had been cut off the place."[33]

Lady Macbeth, trying to rub out the sign of her guilt (while still holding the taper—there was no place to deposit it on the Jacobean stage as there is in modern productions), was a startling image of the captured witch. Her guilt made her act that role as she remembered the sight of "so much blood" streaming from Duncan's body. The image would soon be repeated when John Rice played Lucretia Borgia's repentance scene before *her* death in Barnes's play. Lucretia, too, sees the blood that streamed from her murdered husband, and cries out (lines 2283–88):

> You see in my soul deformed blots.
> Deliver me from that murthered man—
> He comes to stab my soul! I murdered him.
> O Gismond, Gismond, hide those bleeding wounds.
> My soul bleeds drops of sorrow for thy sake.
> Look not so wrathful! I am penitent!

Lucretia has been poisoned by her father, and her penitent death scene is contrasted with his despairing fall into the devil's clutches at the play's conclusion. Unlike Alexander or Faustus, she can still plead for forgiveness (lines 2312–15):

> Merciful Father, let not Thy mercy pass!
> Extend Thy mercy where no mercy was.

Merciful Father, for Thy Son's dear merit
Pardon my sinful soul. Receive my spirit.

Expirat Lucrece.

Shakespeare is more subtle than Barnes; but his sinning lady is also shown in penitent collapse, tortured by guilt and visions of blood. The pity of the physician, with his own hope for mercy, states indirectly the themes made blatant by Barnes: "Yet I have known those which have walk'd in their sleep who have died holily in their bed . . . God! God! Forgive us all!" (5.1.59–61, 75). It is a hope Macbeth, sealed up in the false confidence of his witches' assurance, has long ago forfeited. He must end like Pope Alexander, or Doctor Faustus—beyond repentance, defiant to the end.

five

Jesuits

equivocation of the fiend

I ask the reader to cast his or her mind back to the analogy I used in the first chapter, comparing the Gunpowder Plot to a plan of communist saboteurs in the 1950s. Imagine not only that a communist cell was apprehended, with nuclear materials for blowing up the Capitol, but that a communist handbook was captured as well, one that spelled out all the evil doctrines communists were accused of espousing. This imagined book gave instructions on how to infiltrate democratic institutions, using lies and plausible "covers" for gaining positions from which the whole governmental structure could be undermined from within.

King James's investigators claimed they had found just such a guide to the dismantling of royal government in England. It was called *A Treatise of Equivocation*. It had been circulated among Catholics in manuscript, and a copy of it was found in the chambers of one of the lay Plotters, Francis Tresham.[1] The treatise's author was called by the Royal Chaplain "a kind of priest of Satan" (*sacerdos quidam Satanae*), since the work described how the Sovereign's officers might be deceived, even under oath.[2] This, it was said, destroyed all hope of honest dealings between James and his subjects. It abused the nature of language, perverting it the way witchcraft undid other natural things.

The Jesuit quandary with regard to truth is one shared by all persecuted believers. If one is forced to practice one's religion in secret, how far can one go in keeping the secret? The priests moved about in disguise, pretending not to be priests. Could they *say* they were not priests, if asked? For some time, this troubled the Jesuits, who sought advice from their superiors in Rome. In time, they elaborated rules for hiding the truth—just as Jewish believers in fifteenth-century Spain had, or secret Protestants ("Nicodemists") in Catholic countries.[3]

The problem of answering legitimate authority truthfully arose, in 1581, with the trial of Edmund Campion, the first Jesuit to be captured in England. Campion refused to answer what he called "bloody questions," ones that he could not answer without, in effect, committing suicide. This was an early effort to assert a right against self-incrimination.[4] The right was expressly claimed by Francis Tresham when he was questioned about harboring Campion. Tresham said that "To betray oneself [*seipsum prodere*] is contrary to the law of nature."[5]

The next Jesuit to be caught and executed (in 1595) was the poet Robert Southwell, turned in by a woman, Anne Bellamy, who said he had instructed her on how to lie in good conscience if asked whether she had harbored Southwell. Southwell asked his accusers if they would answer truthfully men who asked where Queen Elizabeth was so they could murder her. This does not seem a moral problem to us—who would hesitate to lie to Nazis searching for hidden Jews? But the tradition of moral theology was absolutist on the matter of lying, depending heavily on Saint Augustine's doctrine that one can *never* lie.[6] The view of language as natural, not artificial, was still held in the sixteenth century. God had *named* creatures as he made them. Either he named them himself ("And God called the light Day, and the darkness he called Night," Genesis 1.5) or he delegated the naming to Adam ("and whatsoever Adam called every living creature, that was the name thereof," Genesis 2.19).[7] To give false names, to pervert language, was a sin against nature. Abusing words was abusing things—that was one source of the potency of abused language in magic and witchcraft. It explains why it was so easy for controversialists to equate Jesuits with witches.

Garnet wrote his *Treatise* to defend Southwell's instructions to Anne Bellamy, since Southwell said she could tell an apparent (not a real) lie by the practice of "mental reservation." One could not conceive or hold a conscious falsehood; but, one could convey the truth in part, or by different media. Given a proposition, "God is not unjust," one can *say* "God is not" and then *write* "unjust," or say "unjust" by sign language, or in a foreign tongue unknown to one's hearer—or even say it "in one's mind." The proposition in itself is the same, no matter how it is expressed, in whole or in part. God knows the truth of the proposition, and he knows that one is mentally formulating that truth. Garnet quoted Saint Gregory as saying: "Men judge a man's heart by his words. God judges words by the heart."[8] The truth must always be first formulated in God's presence (*in ordine ad Deum*), and any partial expression is broken off as if by accident. (Struck dead between saying "God is not" and "unjust," one would not be guilty of a falsehood.) The claim that equivocators spoke only *in ordine ad Deum* makes the Porter say that *his* equivocator committed treason "for God's sake" (2.3.10).

Garnet put severe limits around equivocation in general, and around mental reservation in particular. There are some cases where one can never use it (to deny one's faith, to advance an evil cause, to hurt others, to promote any act of itself sinful). One should not use mental reservation unless forced to (to protect fellow believers, to resist unjust aggression). It is better to use truthful evasion, or the use of a legitimate sense of a word which is not the listener's expected sense.[9] Even when adopting an apparently false name, it should be in some sense true—so Jesuits used distant family names, or names indicating place of origin, or former occupation, or even hobby.[10] Garnet called himself "Farmer," a fact that enters into *Macbeth*.

The irony of the equivocation dispute is that the shock expressed on one side, and the ingenuity exercised on the other, came from the same cramped view of language, one we now find naive. The Jesuits were condemned for mental trickery; but as they said themselves, if all they wanted to recommend was *lying*, they could have done that without all the mental exercise. They were scrupulously trying to make sure that whatever they said was *true* (at some level, in some consciously intended sense). But this very regard for truth in a difficult situation branded them as liars. They were equivocal in every way—disguised, pretending to be what they were not, speaking in obscure riddles, lurking in peaceful-looking houses.

Spenser had set the literary tone on Jesuits when he created Malengin (Evil-Deviser), who confounds man "through his sleights," hiding in holes "full of windings" and of "hidden ways." This figure spreads a net "to fish for fools," using "juggling feats" and mysteries of "legerdermain." He varies his shape like Proteus.[11] The Jesuit was a shape-shifter, a doubler, a reverser of things, an overturner. As Dekker put it:

He's brown, he's grey, he's black, he's white—
He's anything! A Jesuite![12]

He wrote that in *The Double P,* and "doubling" was another word for equivocating.[13] *Macbeth*'s witches "palter with us in a *double* sense" (5.8.20). *Macbeth* is full of equivocal, reversible, backward-and-for-warding realities. Days are fair and foul. Malcolm is vicious and virtuous. Morning is night. Witches are male and female. Macduff's son is fathered and fatherless. Drink puts on and puts off. Promises are true and false, and "nothing is / But what is not" (1.3.141–42). The play's labyrinthine ambiguities have been intensively studied, and are often related to Jesuitical equivocation.[14] Not only do the witches use equivocation—called that by Macbeth (5.5.42), but the Porter plays equivocally on the very word "equivocation" while welcoming an equivocator into hell.[15]

If we except a few gibes by Macduff's son, the Porter scene is the only bawdy and comic intrusion into this dark play. It was resented for this, considered unworthy of Shakespeare by Coleridge, though De Quincy defended it as "comic relief." Now the scene is generally related to the diabolic aspect of the play by tracing a rather distant connection with the keeping of hell's gate in the Mystery Plays.[16] That tie may have some historical validity, but I doubt that is was actively in the audience's mind. The plying of different trades in hell was a commonplace of comedy—Greene had hell's tapster in *Friar Bacon,* and Dekker has hell's brothel-keeper in *A Knightly Conjuring* and hell's porter in *The Double P* (which, since it is not a play, lacks the obvious tie to the Mysteries).[17]

The diabolic aspects of the scene are brought out by its resem-blance to the witches' first encounter with Macbeth—a relationship probably underscored for the first audience by Robert Armin's acting of the Porter's role *and* the First Witch.[18] The witches greet Macbeth with three hails, three titles. The Porter welcomes three people who come into *his* toils with three titles (instead of names)—farmer, equivocator, English tailor.[19] It would be appropriate to have him circle (to the left) his imagined victims as the witches had first circled Macbeth (hedging him off from Banquo) in a preliminary "damnation" to match the Porter's comic dealings with the damned. The Porter calls on three devils—though he forgets the name of the last one. The witches first responded to their three familiars, though the last one is not named. The Porter scene is a reverse conjuration. The witches circle and make triple invocations to raise spirits from hell. The Porter draws people down to hell.[20]

The Porter's savage humor, close to that of the witches, is established by his choice of three imagined "guests." The first one has often been connected with Henry Garnet because his widely publicized indictment included "Farmer" among his pseudonyms. But some find this confusing, since the second "guest" is the equivocator, and *he* should be Garnet. The solution to the problem must be sought in what the Porter says about all three sinners. He begins (2.3.4–6):

> Here's a farmer, that hang'd himself on th' expectation of plenty come in time. Have napkins enow about you? Here you'll sweat for it.

The reasons for my punctuation will become clear in a moment. The main thing to recognize at the outset is that nothing the Porter says has much, if anything, to do with Father Garnet, according to all prior suggestions for the passage's meaning. The second thing is that *no* suggested meaning made much sense, comic or otherwise. Those who punctuate "Come in time!" have little meaning to give these words. "In time" for what? To be burnt, according to Brooke. But any time would do for that. And what are the napkins? A rich man's handkerchiefs according to Brooke. A handkerchief the farmer used to hang himself according to Delius in the Variorum (a fairly large handkerchief, obviously; about the size of a flag). And, finally, why should a man hang himself for fear of a large harvest? Becuase he thinks it might drive down prices, according to most editors.

Suppose, for a moment, that the farmer is Garnet. He hanged himself in the sense that he came to England on a desperate mission and knew he would be hanged if he were caught. Such a mission looks suicidal to the unsympathetic. What has the harvest to do with such a mission? The Jesuits liked to cite scriptural passages that called priests fishers for men, harvesters of souls. Spenser, as we have seen, portrayed the Jesuitical Malengin as spreading nets to catch souls. The Bible that Shakespeare read and quoted most in his plays, the Bishop's Bible, renders Matthew 9.37 this way:

> The harvest is plenteous, but the laborers are few. Pray ye, therefore, the Lord of the harvest that he will send laborers into his harvest.[21]

The "plenteous" is echoed in the Porter's "expectation of *plenty.*" The harvest that will come eventually made Garnet hope for a plenty that would "come in time."

The Porter sees a figure arriving with handkerchiefs. Why? Handkerchiefs were associated with the public execution of Jesuits, since the emptying of all a man's blood in the savage disemboweling, castrating, and quartering of the hanged bodies of traitors prompted pious Catholics to dip handkerchiefs and other bits of cloth in the martyrs' saving blood.[22] These relics were cherished, and some Catholics held that miracles were worked by them. Samuel Harsnett, in the work on Jesuit exorcisms that is one of the few contemporary books we can prove that Shakespeare read, mocked this belief in the power of "silken twists." He says older superstitions worked miracles with bits of the cross of Jesus, but not of his clothes—yet Catholics do not take any blood-soaked wood from the gallows at Tyburn, just clothes or sops for blood, just a "girdle or twist."[23] The picture of people trying to sop up blood for relics with handkerchiefs, or any cloth at hand, was so vivid and memorable from the public executions that Shakespeare made it the basis of an imagined scene in *Julius Caesar* (one not in Plutarch, his source). Decius reinterprets Calpurnia's fearful dream of Caesar spouting blood into a picture of *saving* blood (*Julius Caesar* 2.2.83–90):

> This dream is all amiss interpreted.
> It was a vision fair and fortunate.
> Your statue spouting blood in many pipes,
> In which so many smiling Romans bath'd,
> Signifies that from you great Rome shall suck
> Reviving blood, and that great men shall press
> For tinctures, stains, relics, and cognizance.

The cognizance was the "colors" worn as an emblem by a man's followers.

So the Porter imagines Farmer Garnet arriving in hell with some of his signature bloody handkerchiefs—which will not work miracles in hell but can be used to wipe his sweat as he is toasted by the "everlasting bonfire." The satire is very close in tone to that of Harsnett, and fits perfectly the mood of victory after the close escape from the Gunpowder Plot.

All the other Plotters had died by the time Garnet reached the scaffold on May 1, 1606. Eight laymen had been hanged, drawn and quartered in London, on separate days that handled four bodies each. A Jesuit brother had died under torture (supposed to be illegal in common law, but used to answer the great threat of the Plot). A Jesuit priest, Edward Oldcorne, was taken to Richmond and executed there. That left Garnet, the putative mastermind of the Plot, for a spectacular last show of retribution. He had been tortured, tried, and questioned after trial, to gather as much information as could be used to discredit him and his religious order. His execution was staged on a special scaffold, between the old (Gothic) Saint Paul's and the mansion of the Bishop, the same place where the victory over the Armada had been celebrated. The spot was chosen to link the threat and the delivery from two major Catholic aggressions.[24] Governing was itself a form of theater in Shakespeare's day.

Garnet was given a chance to repent, as clergy and civil officers continued to question him on the way to the jammed square and up onto the scaffold. Urged to endorse his own confession of complicity in the plot, he said he had confessed only to hearing about the Plot under the seal of confession. "You do but equivocate," he was told—persisting in his sin at the last moment when he could save his soul.[25] Like a Faustus, like Pope Alexander in Barnes's play, Garnet was represented as going off to hell defiant.

As Garnet steps off the scaffold straight into hell, here is the Porter to welcome him (2.3.8–11):

Faith, here's an equivocator!—that could swear in both scales against either scale; who committed treason enough for God's sake, yet could not equivocate to heaven. Oh, come in, equivocator!

Pitting two meanings against each other, so that he cannot be pinned down to either one taken singly—that is the charge against the Jesuit. And doing it *in ordine ad Deum,* in God's eyes and "for God's sake," adds sacrilege to mendaciousness. When the equivocation is used to commit treason—the Powder Treason itself—then there is no way for such equivocation to lead to heaven. The Porter knows *this* sinner has arrived with the right credentials for entry into his hell.

But how can Garnet be both the farmer and the equivocator? For an answer to that puzzle, H. L. Rogers supplies the best evidence in his discussion of the third sinner who arrives in hell. The commentators have heavy going as they try to explain (2.3.8.12–15):

> Faith, here's an English tailor!—come hither for stealing out of a French hose. Come in, tailor! Here you may rest your goose.

Most editors claim that the tailor is going to hell for scanting material on a customer, taking material from a puffy hose, or (to show his stinginess) from a skintight hose—the French hose is made one or the other of these opposites. The "goose" is a smoothing iron, which hell-fire will keep warm now. Not much of a sin for the climactic place in the Porter's catalogue, and not much of a joke for Armin to wring some laughs from.

Rogers takes us into a whole different arena of references, into the controversy over Garnet's miracles. The Catholics sought relics from the scaffold, in their own pious version of the way witches took body parts from the gallows. A person took one of Campion's fingers away from his execution. After that, the authorities kept people away from the dismantled limbs of the quartered priests. But there could be no containment of the blood, where so much was being shed. (As Lady Macbeth says, "Who would have thought the old man to have had *so much* blood in him.") Campion's bloody "girdle" (rope-belt) became an especially prized and wonder-working relic.

In Garnet's case, blood splashed onto a stalk of grain was supposed to have formed a face—his own face—on the grain. The government took special measures to discredit this miracle story, trying to complete the vilification of all Jesuits in Garnet's disgrace. On November 25, 1606, six months after Garnet's death (a month or two, most likely, before *Macbeth*'s performance) the Archbishop of Canterbury called for the Chief Justice to arrest a man for spreading tales of miracles wrought by "Garnet's straw." A hunt was made for the straw to discredit it.[26] On November 27, the Archbishop examined a man whose wife had held the straw in her keeping. The man was re-examined on December 5, and became sufficiently notorious to figure in three stanzas of a satirical poem on Garnet's straw published early in 1607.

The man being examined was a tailor, and the poem refers to the way "a skipping silkman" took the straw to his wife. Although the husband, "a poor plain goseman," did not see the face of Garnet on the straw, a visitor to his home, stealing to its hiding place, *painted* the image, thus fooling tailor and wife. The tailor's (goseman's) "goose" is in the Porter's speech, along with a "skipping silkman" (seller of French hose) and the verb "steal."[27] The tailor was not dead by the time Shakespeare's play was put on, so he cannot himself be meant as the third sinner. Rather, Garnet, as the man whose face appeared on the straw, is greeted once more by the Porter. The whole incident stands for him and his influence, as did the bloody handkerchiefs of the first greeting.

The Porter has greeted Garnet under three titles, just as the witches greeted the same man three times, as Thane of Glamis, Thane of Cawdor, and King thereafter. The multiple greeting is easier to make to Garnet since his straw was supposed to have two images of him, one face contained in the other face's beard.[28] This, too, was mocked in *The Jesuits' Miracles:*

> Rightly to paint the painter well knew how,
> For Garnet had two faces in one hood.
> Equivocation his double face did cloak.
> Equivocating, himself at last did choke.

Rogers's thesis has important implications for the dating of *Macbeth*. Leeds Barroll has suggested that the interest in equivocation might be dying out by Christmas time of 1606, seven months after Garnet's death.[29] But there was a new scandal about Garnet caused by tales of his "miracle," which made the Archbishop of Canterbury start a public hunt for the straw at the end of November and prosecute it on into December. *Macbeth* would have been written just as this new flareup of interest in Garnet was presenting a threat to the official disposition of the Plot and its Plotters. Catholics were supposed to have learned to disassociate themselves from Garnet and the Jesuits. If the legend of Garnet's holiness were allowed to spread, it would be an affront to the official government "line" on the Powder Treason— much like conspiracy theories that challenged the government versions of the attack on Pearl Harbor or the assassination of John Kennedy.

All this would make attacks on Garnet timely.[30] By tracing circles around a spot where he welcomes three images into his toils, the Porter could repeat—at the same spot on the stage—the circles with which the witches first detached Macbeth from Banquo and held the former in the spell of their suggestions. These two encirclements will lead on to the grander weaving of *double* toils about Macbeth in the conjuring scene. Visual associations would underline the connections. The Folio says simply *Enter Porter,* but he would be carrying a light of some sort, both to keep the audience reminded that it is night time and to carry out his function of going to the gate through a dark castle and lighting new parties in. What kind of light would he carry—a lantern, a torch, a taper? Any of these could be used to suggest the fires of hell he imagines himself tending. If a torch or taper, it would suggest a witch, just as Lady Macbeth's taper does in the sleepwalking scene. Armin as Porter and Armin as witch link the scenes of Garnet in hell and Macbeth in the toils of necromancy. The Gunpowder Plot would be suggested in two ways—its menace to the king in Macbeth's regicide, and its failure in the final disposal of traitorous Garnet (safely made the butt of scorn in the Porter scene). "The equivocations of the fiend" are fearful but containable. The proof is the baffling of the Plot by Garnet's defeat.

six

Malcolm

to beguile the time

Readers of the preceding chapter may feel an entirely justified resistance to any reading of Shakespeare that reduces
him to a propagandist. It is clear that he could be fiercely
polemical at times—as in his presentation of La Pucelle during the
anti-Catholic aftermath of the Armada invasion. But his general aim
is to make contemporary excitement work to the advantage of his art.
The play, after all, *is* the thing all else must serve. There are attacks on
Garnet and his equivocation in *Macbeth*. But there are other things
that put the attack in a more complex, ambiguous, and—yes—
equivocal light.

It is clear, for instance, that the King and his officers used deception in order to convict Garnet of being deceitful. If Jesuits lurked in
disguise, so did some of their "pursuivants." The more zealous
Elizabethan priest-hunters, like Sir Francis Walsingham or Richard
Topcliffe, could not quite say, with Macbeth, "There's not a one of
them but in his house / I keep a servant fee'd" (3.4.130–31), but they

were working on it. And Robert Cecil carried the effort over into James's reign.[1]

With the King's complicity, the imprisoned Garnet was duped into secret conferences with his Jesuit confederate, Edward Oldcorne, where witnesses listened in. Some Plotters facing trial were tricked into believing that their confederates had confessed. That may look like nothing more than good police work now, but it seems odd that the people who told lies to uncover evidence against the Plotters should stand up in prosecution and denounce the Plotters for telling lies.

It matters, naturally, who is doing the lying. *Quod licet Jovi non licet bovi.* Kings and clowns have not the same license. The worst charge against the Plotters was that they lied (under oath) to legitimate superiors. The King's men, by contrast, *were* the legitimate authority, the ones giving the oaths, not the ones taking them. The permissibility of using Machiavellian tools against Machiavellians was explored even by moralizing princes like James. He advised his son not to trust untested men; and testing them might call for some role-playing: "Be homely [intimate] or strange with them as you think their behavior deserveth and their nature may bear with."[2] In the Polonius vein, he might even advise the Prince "by indirections [to] find directions out" (*Hamlet* 2.1.63). James's own stratagems and role-playing have made generations of writers see him as the "Duke of dark corners" in *Measure for Measure:* "Craft against vice I must apply" (3.2.277).[3] James would certainly have endorsed Prospero's belated criticism of the ruler who shows a simple-minded trust (*Tempest* 1.2.93–96):

> my trust,
> Like a good parent, did beget of him

A falsehood, in its contrary as great
As my trust was.

A good but naive king like Henry VI can do more harm to his realm than might a crafty Bolingbroke. Lady Macbeth's advice in crime can be turned around and made the counsel of good rule (1.5.63–66):

To beguile the time,
Look like the time—bear welcome in your eye,
Your hand, your tongue; look like th'innocent flower
But be the serpent under 't.

After all, the advice to be "wise as a serpent" is ascribed to Jesus (Matthew 10.16), and devious means were felt to be especially necessary when dealing with covert foes of great ingenuity. One must fight Jesuitical fire with fire.

Yet there was a reluctance to do this, hedged in by the view on language noticed in the preceding chapter. In some of his moods, James was fond of scriptural prescriptions like Matthew 5.37: "Let your communications be, Yea, yea; Nay, nay." He began his first address to Parliament, in 1603, with a promise to show his mind more by action than by words, since "I did ever naturally so mislike a tongue too smooth."[4] And he ended by saying that his words, when he had to rely on them, would be as simple in meaning as he could make them:

It becometh a king, in my opinion, to use no other eloquence than plainness and sincerity. By plainness, I mean that his speeches should be so clear and void of all ambiguity that they may not be thrown or rent asunder in contrary senses, like the old oracles of the pagan gods. And by sincerity, I understand that uprightness and honesty which ought to be in a king's whole speeches and actions—that, as far as a king is in *honor* erected above any of his subjects, so far should he strive in *sincerity* to be above them all; and that his tongue should be ever the true messenger of his head.[5]

Reconciling that code with the need to be crafty as a serpent was no easy matter. How, in *Macbeth,* is Malcolm to stay alive and to plan the rescue of his country when environed by spies ("There's not a one of them / But in his house I keep a servant fee'd," 3.4.130–31) and fending off deceits and feints ("Devilish Macbeth / By many of these trains hath sought to win me," 4.3.117–18)? The testing of loyalties, the anticipation of plots, the foiling of malice test all a prince's cleverness. That can be seen in each of the Gunpowder plays—in fact, the scene of Malcolm's mental fencing with Macduff should be staged with a view to some of those other discussions of trust and deceit.

In *Sophonisba,* when a regicidal plot calls for the breaking of oaths, casuistry insists (2.1.60–61) that

> State shapes are soldered up with base, nay faulty
> (Yet necessary) functions. Some *must* lie.

But Sophonisba defends oaths with the doctrine of James's first address to Parliament (2.1.118–19):

> Speech makes us men, and there's no other bond
> 'Twixt man and man but words.

As Coke argued, against the Jesuit's unsocial use of false language: "The law and sanction of nature hath, as it were, married the heart and tongue, by joining and knitting of them together in a certain kind of marriage; and therefore when there is a discord between these two, the speech that proceeds from them is said to be conceived in adultery."[6]

The man chosen by Marston's plotters as an assassin is a Fawkes-figure, "an engineer long tried for plots" (2.1.71)—but when he finds himself unable to go on, his masters pretend he was only being tested: "We did it but to try / What sense thou hadst of blood" (2.3.23–24). Actually, they have tried him and found him wanting—so *he* is killed.

In *The Devil's Charter*, Barnes has two scenes of princes' testing each other for politic deceitfulness. In the first, Pope Alexander cooperates with one son, Caesar, in catechizing his other son, "Candy" (the Duke of Gandía), to the ways of the world. Caesar says to Candy: "Your heart is too much spic'd with honesty" (439). Which is like Lady Macbeth's words on Macbeth's nature: "It is too full o' th' milk of human kindness" (1.5.17). The Pope instructs his son in dissimulation, a favored synonym of equivocation:

> Lively dissemble faith and holiness
> With clemency, the milk of majesty. [480–81]

In the other scene of vicious catechizing, the Pope accuses Caesar of killing Candy (a secret Alexander learned by necromancy), and the son reponds with accusations concerning the Pope's incest and pederasty. Having probed each other's depths, they gleefully join forces to attack their foes. The Pope exclaims (line 2129):

> A triple joy succeeds a single grief![7]

In *The Whore of Babylon*, those who recruit assassins for the Queen test the candidates' willingness with casuistical processes. They are, as one prospect says, "full of ambage," or ambiguity (3.2.134). Suppose, says one agent, an army with both friends and foes in it, and the need to kill the army's captain for the good of eliminating the foes (3.2.132–33):

> This captain's life, away, might bring this good—
> Of two sides to make one, and save much blood.

In an especially interesting scene of mental fencing, a temptor delicately tries to suggest treason to Campion ("Campeius" in the play) without fully showing his hand until he knows Campeius's readiness to play the game. Campeius fends him off, not wanting to expose his own guilt until he is sure of the other's. The temptor says (2.2.34–36):

> Nothing hath pass'd me,
> I hope, against my country or the state
> That any can take hold of.

Campeius replies:

> If they could,
> 'Tis but mine *aye* to your *no.*

The clever Campeius says the man must come nearer with his meaning and his offer (2.2.88–91):

> What flight soever
> Your words make through this air (though it be troubled),
> Mine ear, sir, is no reaching fowling-piece.
> What passes through, it kills. [2.2.88–91]

Only after long exchanges of mutual distrust do they reach an evil meeting of the minds.

Shakespeare's contemporaries clearly enjoyed these battles of wit, mutual attempts to entrap or to influence indirectly. Characters in the plays perform what T. F. Wharton calls "moral experiments" on each other, where the guinea pigs are also the experimenters.[8] The Malcolm-Macduff scene is the supreme example of this moral experimentation.

Modern directors often welcome the chance, when the play moves to England, to introduce one sequence of brightness, of relief from the oppressive Scottish atmosphere. But that gets the scene off on the wrong foot entirely. The Malcolm we find in this scene is distrustful, harried, on guard. Macbeth's power extends to him with every Scottish emissary. No one is to be trusted. Malcolm has been on the run since we last saw him scurrying from the site of his father's murder, when he told his brother "where we are, / There's daggers in men's smiles" (2.3.139–40). Though the stage direction for Act Four, Scene Three reads only *"Enter Malcolm and Macduff,"* stage hirelings probably served as Malcolm's body guard. He cannot trust himself alone with one who may be an assassin for Macbeth. He tells us in this scene that Macbeth has used many clever tricks to lure him back into the country (4.3.117–19). Failing that, the tyrant may have sent Macduff to kill him. Malcolm bristles with suspicion: "What I *believe*, I'll wail, / What *know*, believe" (4.3.8–9). He thinks Macduff's children are being held hostage by Macbeth until he completes his mission (4.3.26–28):

> Why in that rawness left you wife and child,
> Those precious motives, those strong knots of love,
> Without leave-taking?

(In the source, Macduff flees Scotland only after his children are slain. Shakespeare leaves their fate unknown to increase Malcolm's suspicion. If the murder of Macduff's wife and children were already reported, Malcolm's suspicion would seem unjustified.)

The first thing to notice about this scene is its ritual nature. Malcolm makes three charges against himself, and Macduff makes three formal answers of roughly the same length. Then, when Macduff has passed the test, Malcolm abjures each of his charges, leaving Macduff bewildered by the whole manipulative process ("Such welcome and unwelcome things at once / 'Tis hard to reconcile," 138–39). The testing of a person by three trials is a folktale theme, often brought into art—the test of the three caskets in *The Merchant of Venice* or the three riddles in *Turandot*. What sets this scene apart is that *we* are testing the prince as *he* tests the suspect. Malcolm's ability to rule, not Macduff's good faith, is the thing to be established for the audience. In this he is contrasted with Duncan, who presumed people's allegiance too easily, who had no sense of the affront some would feel at his promotion of Malcolm to the Earlship of Cumberland. Now this Malcolm, whose life was saved in the opening battle of the play (1.2.3–5), must save himself by shrewdness, suspicion, and pre-emptive challenges to those who would get near him.

The tension of the scene must come from the way each man feels out the other, exactly as Campeius and his temptor do in *The Whore of Babylon*—though the latter men are looking for sure signs of vice in each other, while Malcolm and Macduff try to see if there is hidden virtue. This guardedness of language, this chary and tentative mode, makes editors misread Malcolm's foxy opening ploy (4.3.13–17). After calling Macbeth a tyrant, he goes on to say that Macbeth

> Was once thought honest—you have lov'd him well;
> He hath not touch'd you yet. I am young, but something

> You may discern of him through me, and wisdom
> To offer up a weak, poor, innocent lamb
> T' appease an angry God.

We are told that this means: "Since Macbeth has not personally offended your earlier love, you may seek some advantage from him in me, though I am young, if you offer me up to him as a lamb." There are many problems with that.

For one thing, it makes no sense for Malcolm to draw attention to his youth as if that had anything (negative or positive) to do with his serviceability as a sacrifice to Macbeth. It is not Malcolm's age that matters but his title (Cumberland) and lineage. That would make him a danger to Macbeth—and therefore a welcome sacrifice—no matter what his age.

Another problem is the presentation of Macbeth as "an angry god." He has just been called a tyrant whose very name blisters the tongue. A third problem—and the most important one for setting the tone of the scene—is Malcolm's presentation of himself as an innocent lamb. He is about to paint himself as more tyrannous than Macbeth; and though he reasserts his innocence after that trial-by-falsehood, the picture of Malcolm as a lamb is what makes the character so uninteresting in most productions.

How, then, should this passage be read? *As mocking Macduff's moralism.* The "angry god" is the lord of retribution Macduff appeals to for saving Scotland. Malcolm is saying: "You get along with a man who earlier seemed honest. I am young (as Macbeth was in his 'honest' days), but you can see the possibilities of later evil in me, as in him, and you can see what (little) wisdom it is to offer him—or me—up as a lamb to your disapproving God." (Editors beg the question when they print "God" with a lower case g. The "angry god" for righting Scotland's wrongs is—God.)

Malcolm has already begun the testing of Macduff by presenting *himself* as a villain. To understand what that involves, we must ask, more precisely than previous commentators have, just what the test consists of. Malcolm is usually presented as painting himself black and saying—what? That he will not take the crown because he is unworthy, he is too evil? If Malcolm is as evil as he says, what virtue makes him refuse to put a bad man on the throne? He says he is a grasping fellow—and therefore he will not grasp. Avaricious—so will not aspire.

Malcolm puts himself in the position of Campeius's temptor in Dekker's play—recruiting another to evil while making his overtures in a veiled way: "I am worse than Macbeth—will you follow me" (as Malcolm presumes he is villainously following Macbeth)? This approach entirely changes the dynamics of the scene. As normally performed, Malcolm's self-accusations are unconvincing to the audience, as they should be to Macduff. But if Malcolm has already directed Macduff to "discern something of Macbeth through me," there is a wink-and-leer indirection to the whole scene.

When Malcolm describes Macbeth, there should not be a censoriousness at odds with boasts of his *own* villainy, but a kind of connoisseurship in vice. Malcolm goes over the catalogue of sins like an admiring colleague and competitor (4.3.57–60):

> I grant him bloody,
> Luxurious, avaricious, false, deceitful,
> Sudden, malicious, smacking of every sin
> That has a name.[9]

But Malcolm has sins no one has yet named: "There's no bottom, none / In my voluptuousness" (4.3.60–61). The tone is that of Richard III topping rivals in vice at *III Henry VI* 3.2.188–93:

> I'll play the orator as well as Nestor,
> Deceive more slily than Ulysses could,
> And like a Sinon, take another Troy.
> I can add colors to the chameleon,
> Change shapes with Proteus for advantages,
> And set the murtherous Machevil to school.[10]

The triple test made of Macduff is in Holinshed's chronicle, Shakespeare's source, though Shakespeare has made the situation more complex and subtle (by, for instance, giving Malcolm cause to think Macduff complicitous with Macbeth, since the death of Macduff's family is unknown in the play). One change in the source seems surprising. Holinshed organizes the accusations Malcolm directs to himself in this mounting list: lust, avarice, *and dissimulating*.[11] This tells us how grave was the charge of lying speech; Shakespeare, one expects, would want to keep that charge in a play so concerned with equivocation and dissembled meanings. But Shakespeare changed the last item, so that his list is: lust, avarice, *and general evil*. Why the change? H. L. Rogers argued that equivocation was so bad that Malcolm could not accuse himself of it even in a feigned way:

> I do not believe that Shakespeare could have made the stage Malcolm speak of himself in the terms used by Holinshed's Malcolm; dissimulation had become such a dirty word that it could not then be used of the "good" king and ancestor of James.[12]

But Malcolm accuses himself of a diabolical desire to dismantle the universe (lines 97–100). It is hard to see why he should hesitate to lay claim to the supreme diabolical symbol of that period.

In fact, the hyperbolical nature of Malcolm's last evil boast explains why Shakespeare does not confine the charge to the one (admittedly heinous) sin used as a climax to Holinshed's list. The playwright had more direct ways of tying this scene to the Jesuitical schemes of Gunpowder malevolence. The tempting of Macduff with ambiguous speeches, meant to lead him on, repeats the tempting of Macbeth with ambiguous predictions in the heath and necromancy scenes. All involve a triple exchange between the temptor and the trial subject. This resemblance should be brought out in the staging. As the Porter's greeting to his threefold sinners was a kind of reverse conjuring (calling spirits *down*, not *up*), so Malcolm's trial of Macduff is a reverse of the corrupting process. The witches trammeled Macbeth in ambition's foils. Malcolm strips away the appearance of Macduff's complicity in Macbeth's evil. The shrewd king undoes evil magic with a heavenly cleverness like James's in seeing through the ambiguities of the Plotters' language.

But Malcolm first weaves an evil illusion before dispelling it. He circles Macduff to make his ritual three claims to vice, moving to the left as the witches (and the Porter) did. When the trial is over, he reverses the spell, moving to the right as he takes off each of the mock curses laid on himself. He must "unspeak" the spell, abjure what he said—as Prospero and Faustus "abjure" their magic (*Tempest* 5.1.51; *Faustus* A2.1.8). Malcolm says, in lines 123–31, that he can

> Unspeak mine own detraction, here abjure
> The taints and blames I laid upon myself,

> For strangers to my nature. I am yet
> Unknown to woman, never was forsworn,
> Scarcely have coveted what was mine own,
> At no time broke my faith, would not betray
> The Devil to his fellow, and delight
> No less in truth than life—my first false speaking
> Was this upon myself.

This reverse spell shows that Malcolm did include forswearing, breaking faith, and false speaking—i.e., dissimulation—in the general indictment of himself.

Why, then, did he not focus on that expressly? Because the hyperbole of the last charge is meant to call up the confusion of order by magic reversals and conjuring. Malcolm gives us a "shorter-catechism" version of Macbeth's great conjuring speech. Macbeth would "confound" navigation in directionless storm, tumble nature's germens all together, till destruction sicken. In lines 98–100, Malcolm would

> Pour the sweet milk of concord into hell,
> Uproar the universal peace, confound
> All unity on earth.

These "confoundings" remind us that confusion is the mark of Babylon/Rome/Hell.[13] The climax of Malcolm's temptation makes him a false conjurer—perhaps wearing a large cloak like the one Ben Jonson disguised himself in when *he* wanted to pose as a conjurer.[14]

The conjuring atmosphere of the trial is cleared, and poetically exorcised, by Malcolm's description of the good magic of a providentially favored king. Malcolm's own model is not Macbeth but "Edward the Confessor," his new ally. As he explains to Macduff (in lines 147–59), there is

Malcolm

A most miraculous work in this good king
Which often, since my here-remain in England,
I have seen him do. How he solicits heaven,
Himself best knows; but strangely-visited people,
All swol'n and ulcerous, pitiful to the eye,
The mere despair of surgery, he cures,
Hanging a golden stamp about their necks,
Put on with holy prayers; and, 'tis spoken,
To the succeeding royalty he leaves
The healing benediction. With this strange virtue
He hath a heav'nly gift of prophecy,
And sundry blessings hang about his throne
That speak him full of grace.

This long speech has been criticized as extraneous to the play's action. But the Gunpowder Plot, and James's supposed role in discovering it, give special force to a line like "He hath a heav'nly gift of prophecy." Besides, Malcolm's reverence for Edward tells us a great deal about his own character. We have first watched him prove a skilled physician of the soul in probing, diagnosing, and "curing" Macduff. He will prove the same kind of healer to his native land. Caithness says of him (5.2.27–29):

Meet we the med'c'ner of the sickly weal,
And with him pour we, in our country's purge,
Each drop of us.[15]

This marks the great contrast with Macbeth. So far from physicking his kingdom—from curing subjects as Edward does—Macbeth cannot find another who will "minister to a mind diseased" (5.3.40). Like his wife, Macbeth "more needs the divine than the physician"

(5.1.74); but he is beyond such ministrations. He hopes for an anodyne instead of a real cure ("some sweet oblivious antidote," 5.3.43). As for the country, he wishes the physician would do what he as king should have done (5.3.50–52):

> If thou couldst, doctor, cast
> The water of my land, find her disease,
> And purge it to a sound and pristine health.

The reverent atmosphere around Edward's cures is contrasted with Macbeth's "Throw physic to the dogs!" (5.3.47). The entry of the doctor before Malcolm's speech can be staged to mark a similarity with the doctor's entry to Macbeth. The false witch-magic and true cure by prayer are at the separate poles of political action. Edward prevails by orisons, not oracles ("How he solicits heaven / Himself best knows . . . Put on with holy prayers").

Only at this point is the spell of witchcraft in the play finally broken. Ross's arrival plunges the Scots back into the reported misery of their country, but Malcolm becomes a physician to Macduff's grief for his wife and children.[16] First he prescribes a "purgative" of words (4.3.209–10):

> Give sorrow words. The grief that does not speak
> Whispers the o'er-fraught heart, and bids it break.

Then he administers a roborative (lines 214–15):

> Let's make us med'cines of our great revenge
> To cure this deadly grief.

It is true that Malcolm is manipulative here, as in the testing scenes. He is fashioning Macduff into an instrument of his purpose. His staccato clauses brisk up Macduff (lines 228–29):

Malcolm

> Be this the whetstone of your sword. Let grief
> Convert to anger. Blunt not the heart. Enrage it.

The shrewd manipulator is far closer to James's image of himself than is the wimp or milksop Malcolm so often seen on the stage. Malcolm only takes his proper station in the play if we see him as the great counter-witch pitted against Macbeth. He has "purged" and strengthened Macduff. Now he launches him at the target, "devilish Macbeth."

seven

Macbeth

outrun the pauser

L ady Macbeth asks of her evil spirits that they make her insensitive (stopping up the passages of remorse, 1.5.44), and she is relieved to see that wine contributes to that useful deadening (2.2.1). Macbeth wants his own psychic mechanism to be short-circuited. At first he simply observes that "function / Is smother'd" when his surmise leaps toward new possibilities (1.3.140–41). But he soon *desires* that the eye not know what the hand is up to (1.4.52), that events swallow up consequences (1.7.1–4). He marvels that acts could go forward without the spur of thought or decision (1.7.25–28). Once launched into action, he cannot look back (3.4.135–37), and he will not look any farther ahead than to the instant task, too horrible to contemplate, but not too horrible to do without contemplating it. He tells his wife to be innocent of such knowledge (3.2.45) and so far as possible keeps himself innocent of it. Bad must be treated homeopathically with further bad (3.2.55). Such cures "must be acted ere they may be scanned" (3.4.139). The first conception of the heart must leap to the hand, no sooner thought than acted (4.1.146–49).

He wants to leap into action automatically, to preclude fear, hesitation, or conscience—and he succeeds so well that the short-circuited parts of him atrophy, like an unused limb: "I have almost forgot the taste of fears" (5.5.9). He has tried to skip past time at will, out-tricking it. "Time, thou anticipat'st my dread exploits," he lamented at one point (4.1.144). By speeding past time, he has eliminated it. It is no longer articulated with any meaning but mere iteration, mere empty succession (5.5.19–28).

Macbeth engages in a self-refashioning that amounts to sabotage committed upon himself. He systematically disconnects the systems of reflection. He even has a short-circuited phrase to describe what he has done to himself: "my strange-and-self-abuse" (3.4.141). It is telling that he explains his actions this way even when he is lying. Asked why he killed the grooms in their sleep, he answers (2.3.110–11):

> Th' expedition of my violent love
> Outrun the pauser, reason.

The jiggering with his own psychic mechanism makes Macbeth's mind move in a blur of images, as if he were on "speed." That makes his speeches hallucinatory, even when he is not seeing the dagger or Banquo's ghost. The words get tangled in their rush from him, in their plunge past obstacles into action. That is why the soliloquies present so many textual problems—far more than cluster in other sections of the play. We must doubt whether the text is sound in some place—unusual language is more apt to be jumbled in transmission. The "packed" quality of the speeches has led to misinterpretation as well as futile revisions.

A good example is the first speech where Macbeth discusses the jump-sequences he would like to introduce into time's flow. If the assassination could be an act *out* of sequence, with no antecedent or consequence, a be-all and end-all in itself, a means to the goal *and* the goal, so that one is contained in the other (a success by mere surcease)—then—what? Then, according to 1.7.5–7 (in the Folio),

here,

But here, upon this bank and school of time,
We'd jump the life to come.

How does one jump from a bank *and* school? Almost all editors adopt Theobald's famous emendation of *school* to *shoal*—disastrously, I believe.

Shoal means shallow water, as in "sounded all the depths and shoals of honor" (*Henry VIII* 3.2.436). How does one jump from the bank *and* the water? Theobald tried to make shoal mean "passage *through* shallow water," or ford: "this shallow, this narrow ford, of human life." So one jumps from the bank to the ford to what? One should *arrive* at the opposite shore, not avoid it, yet "jump" must mean "skip over" or "cancel" here, not jump *to* or achieve. The picture is too jumbled to bear thought.[1]

What can be made of *school* if that is retained? Heath (see Variorum) wanted "bank-and-school" to mean "bench-in-school," which goes nicely with the later "teach bloody instructions" but not so well with "jump the life to come." What help is the physical furniture of a schoolroom to that process (whatever it is)? No one I know of has suspected that the corruption may be in *bank*, not *school*. F's "Banke," with capital B, could well be a setter's misunderstanding of "Ranke." We read at *Lear* 2.4.258 that not being vicious "Stands in some rank [kind or category] of praise." It is the usage that survives in "rank and file." A *rank* of time would be some category of time. School, then, would not be the physical building (with benches in it) but a body of interpretation, like "school of night" at *Love's Labour's* 4.3.251. "*This* rank-and-school of time" would be the kind-and-view of time suggested by what immediately precedes. "This" is a resumptive reference back, not a physical marker.

What was "this" interpretation of time? That it ended each act with the act, rather than leading on to consequences. If one could believe that, then (*upon this view of time*) one could skip or cancel succeeding time. It would be canceled by the surcease of the self-contained act. For *jump* as *skip* or *cancel*, see *Cymbeline* 5.4.179–82: "You must either be directed . . . or jump the after-inquiry on your peril" (another passage having to do with *instruction*).

But then Macbeth reflects that it is not so simple. He wants an exempt time, sealed off from the flow of time, in which to commit a consequence-less murder—like the exempt space marked out by the conjurer's circle, one that seals its ambit off from God's providential order all around the circle. But time flows on into consequential acts: murder calls for retaliation. The interpretation of time as making a single act "the be-all and the end-all here, but here" is not tenable. That "school of time" comes up against the fact that "We still have judgment here" [*not* surcease "here but here"]. We give others "bloody instruction"—to kill in return, just as Campion's "bloody questions" called for a *self*-killing response. The passage should be emphasized this way:

> If it were done when 'tis done, then 'twere well
> It were done quickly. If th' assassination
> Could trammel up the consequence and catch,
> With his surcease, success—that but this blow

> Might be the be-all and the end-all here,
> But here!—upon *this* rank and school of time
> We'd *jump* the life to come. But . . .

This is just the first of three difficult passages in this soliloquy. The second one is the famous "new-born babe" sequence, much discussed and argued over. Cleanth Brooks gave the passage an exhaustive "new criticism" analysis, connecting the babe with every other reference to children or male adulthood in *Macbeth*.[2] Helen Gardner responded that Brooks had made the passage more, not less, obscure.[3] Kenneth Muir tried to reconcile the work of his fellow critics.[4] And the battles go on.

The passage *is* difficult. No phrase in it but has caused problems.

> And pity like a naked new-born babe
> Striding the blast, or heaven's cherubim horsed
> Upon the sightless couriers of the air,
> Shall blow the horrid deed in every eye,
> That tears shall drown the wind.

It may help to take minor points first, since they can give clues to harder matters.

1. How do "tears drown the wind"? Most editors take "drown" to mean "kill by immersion," and conclude that, in Johnson's words, there is "remission of the wind in a shower."[5] That does not seem to be a meteorological fact, and it fits ill the context: passions should be raised, not allayed, by revelation of the regicide. Actually, "drown" can mean simply "drench" or "flood," as in a passage with strong similarities to this one, *Hamlet* 2.2.562ff., where Hamlet says that a real (not a feigned) murder

> would drown the stage with tears,
> And cleave the general ear with horrid speech . . . .

There is no question of *killing* the stage by immersion. So, in our passage, tears will drench the wind, be swirled along in them. *Hamlet's* actor splits ears with horrid speech; *Macbeth's* angels blow the horrid deed in every—eye, not ear. In both cases, horrifying testimony to a crime is delivered.

2. Why are the winds "sightless"? Muir, in his edition, glossed the word as invisible—which is clearly what it means at 1.5.49 (demons' "sightless substance"). But he changed his mind when editing *King Lear*, where winds snatch at Lear's hair "with eyeless rage" (3.1.8). Winds, which make people close their eyes, may be thought of as sightless—*putti* in the corners of old pictures, representing the four winds, sometimes close their eyes while puffing out their checks to blow.

3. How do angels blow a deed into eyes? Portents and apparitions mark the death of kings. The angels can either *cause* these portents, or *be* these portents. If the latter is the case, then the coursers cannot be sightless in the sense of invisible. We are dealing with visual evidence, not acoustic. I mentioned earlier that "blowing" was a charged word in the Gunpowder Plot days, related to the imagined portent of royal limbs flying through the air. The Plot was foiled, and that evidence had to be imagined; but Macbeth is supposing that Duncan's death *does* occur, and he fears what portents will follow. Some portents do, in fact, occur when the murder has been committed—an owl brings down a falcon, and horses go wild (2.4.11–18). The heavens protest what has been done on earth (lines 5–6):

Thou seest the heavens, as troubled with man's act,
Threatens his bloody stage.

Macbeth is imagining some such revelation of the crime from above.

4. What is the division of labor between the babe and the cherubim? None, says Gardner—they are both symbols of innocence. She mocks Brooks's treatment of the babe as Pity and the cherubim as Vengeance. But cherubs can be judges—Hamlet threatens Claudius with the cryptic remark that he (Hamlet) sees a cherub who reads his (Claudius's) mind (4.3.48). Brooks rightly contrasts the babe, whose powerlessness is emphasized (it is not only new-born but naked), with powerful coursers guided by angels. The messengers seem fitted to give different testimony, raising pity *and* fear, just as Hamlet's imagined actor, with his "horrid speech," can "make mad the guilty, and appall the free [from guilt]." Pity is paired by contrast with threats at *Comedy of Errors* 1.1.10 and *Coriolanus* 1.6.36.

5. What is a "naked new-born babe" doing out in a cruel blast of air? The babe stands on the blast, bestrides it in that sense. (The moon bestrides a cloud at *Romeo* 2.2.31 and Margaret says at *III Henry VI* 5.4.31: "Bestride the rock, the tide will wash you off"). The cherubim guide their coursers. The babe just stands helpless in the storm. This is a powerful image, and it was given powerful expression in a poem printed four years before *Macbeth* was performed. Robert Southwell's "The Burning Babe" has these features in common with Shakespeare's image. The babe is "newly born." It "did in the air appear"—cf. "striding the blast." It sheds "floods of tears"—cf. "drown with tears." It makes "mercy blow the coals"—cf. "blow the deed." The babe seems to be naked in the cold—it displays its

"faultless breast." Southwell's poem hangs the Christ child in the air over a wintry Christmas scene to have its heat of love melt the viewer's cold heart. Justice lights fires of vengeance which the babe's melting love puts out—as Shakespeare's babe offers compassion alongside the cherubim's justice. The blood that melts into the fire and puts it out fuses the image of the babe in the air and Christ hung on the cross—another meeting of mercy and justice.

I do not think that Shakespeare is imitating Southwell, but the extraordinary conjunction of similar elements suggests that Shakespeare may have been nudged by Southwell's poem toward this particular symbol of mercy and pity. Shakespeare's babe is not the Christ child. It is Pity in a personified form. But the iconography is the same.[6]

> As I in hoary winter's night
> > Stood shivering in the snow,
> Surpris'd I was with sudden heat
> > Which made my heart to glow.
>
> And lifting up a fearful eye
> > To view what fire was near,
> A pretty Babe all burning bright
> > *Did in the air appear.*
>
> Who, scorched with excessive heat,
> > Such *floods of tears* did shed.
> As though his floods should quench his flames
> > Which with his tears were fed.
>
> "Alas," quoth he, "but *newly born,*
> > In fiery heats I fry;
> Yet none approach to warm their hearts,
> > Or feel my fire, but I.

My faultless breast the furnace is,
   The fuel wounding thorns.
Love is the fire, and sighs the smoke.
   The ashes, shame and scorns.

The fuel Justice layeth on,
   And Mercy *blows the coals.*
The metal, in the furnace wrought,
   Are men's defiled souls—

For which, as now on fire I am
   To work them to this good,
So will I melt into a bath
   To wash them in my blood.

With this he vanish'd out of sight,
   And swiftly shrunk away.
And straight I called unto mind
   That it was Christmas day.[7]

The difficulties in Macbeth's Act One, Scene Seven soliloquy continue to the very end, in these possibly corrupt lines (1.7.25–28):

   I have no spur
To prick the sides of my intent, but only
Vaulting ambition which o'erleaps, itself,
And falls on th' other.

By contrast with the racing cherubim on their couriers, Macbeth is stalled. He cannot prod on his intent. The natural thing is to take *itself* as the object of o'erleaps, though a thing that can jump over itself belongs in the poems of Edward Lear not of William Shakespeare. Ambition needs no spurs—it leaps of itself, unprompted. Compare Ben Jonson, *Catiline* 3.3.161-62 (Regents edition):

though horror leaped, itself,

Into the scale.

What does self-prompting ambition fall on? "The other" is a foe,
and "fall on" means attack:

The bold young men that, when he bids 'em charge,

Fall on like fire.[8]

Ben Jonson uses "go on" in a similar way in *Catiline* 1.1:142-43:

daring as he would

Go on against the gods.

Macbeth says he has no spur to guide a rational intent. All he has—
and he is at the moment too wise to accept it—is a berserk ambition
that spontaneously goes too far (o'erleaps) and attacks anything in
its way (any "other").

The nervous telegraphic style of Macbeth's speech deserves fuller
study; but enough has been looked at to indicate the blowing of his
linguistic fuses as he forces himself on into dreadful action, doing
violence to "the pauser, reason."

In the last act, some of Macbeth's words are obscure. But his
actions also seem mysterious in the Folio text and directions. In Act
Five, Scene Three he asks for his armor, and Seyton says, "'Tis not
needed yet," but Macbeth will put it on anyway. Fourteen lines later
he says, "Come, put my armor on; give me my staff." Six lines after
that: "Pull't off [his armor?], I say." Four lines on: "Bring it [the
armor?] after me." He exits, presumably still unarmed. Not till the
end of Scene Five does he say, "Arm! Arm! And out!" Then, six lines
later, he says: "At least we'll die with harness on our back." Most
directors have Macbeth arm between scenes, but that seems to destroy
the point (whatever it is) of his alternating resolution and reluctance
in arming.[9] What stage business do these various starts and stops
indicate?

Ever since Caroline Spurgeon's 1935 book *Shakespeare's Imagery* drew attention to the language about Macbeth's clothes—too alien, too large, too strange to fit him—directors have tried various ways of suggesting that their actor wears "borrowed robes" (1.3.109). Olivier came out in a large robe in the discovery scene after the murder and tried to "lose" his recently bloodied hands in it.[10] Welles wore a crown that looked too large for his head. Trevor Nunn gave Duncan a huge priest-like cope which is carried or stationed near Macbeth when he is not wearing it, a shining symbol of the kingship he never quite makes his own.

The elaborate business with the armor, the circling of the language back to images of clothing, the general importance of emblematic costume on Shakespeare's stage—and especially of a *king's* emblematic dress—indicate that Macbeth's robing is important. We see him go from soldier to courtier to king to conjurer and back to soldier.

It is instructive to look at other scenes where there is important business having to do with costume. In *The Tempest*, Prospero's cloak is an important prop. He must take it off to speak as a man and father ("Pluck my magic garment from me," 1.2.24) and resume it to compel the spirits. Faustus's cloak was important in Philip Henslowe's inventory (see Frontispiece).[11] The actor Richard Alleyn first appeared as Faustus in clerical garb, a surplice with a cross on his breast.[12] But after his contract with the devil is signed, the evil spirits bring him "rich apparel" and clothe him in it (*Doctor Faustus* A2.1.82–84).

But the most spectacular use of raiment is evident in the *other* play in the Shakespeare troupe's repertory of 1607, Barnes's *The Devil's Charter*. The play opens with Alexander being robed in the panoply of a pope. That the robe is an evil conjurer's is shown by the fact that the devils put it on him and then give him a magic book (like the book

Mephistopheles brings to Faustus). As the chorus of the play put it (lines 70–71):

> Satan, transfigur'd like a protonotary,
> To him makes offer of the triple crown.

Later, when Alexander conjures, he resumes the robe and takes up the book, while telling an acolyte to put on *his* vestments (lines 1851–72). At the end of the play, we see Alexander sitting "unbraced" in his study, trying ineffectually to repent. Then he rises, goes to the curtain over the inner chamber, and pulls it aside—to reveal the devil throned and wearing Alexander's pontificals (lines 3339–42). It is a splendid *coup de théâtre*. Alexander knows he has lost all his power, now that the devil has reclaimed his proper garb (lines 3545–47).

> My robes! My robes! He robs me of my robes!
> Bring me my robes or take away my life!
> My robes, my life, my soul and all, is gone.

Barnes's play is full of references to clothes, to things like Alexander's "cloaking" of his vices.[13] And Caesar, his son, throws off his own clerical robes to show he is wearing armor underneath. The other Gunpowder play of 1606, Dekker's *The Whore of Babylon*, also used papal robes for the Whore's pompous court. Both Dekker and Barnes show the conjunction of papal and witch-like powers in the wizard's cloak.[14] Another attribute of the wizard is his wand, or staff, or rod—the wand we see Faustus wield in the illustration to the 1616 Quarto, the staff Mephistopheles wields at B3.2.16; the staff Prospero must break when he abjures his magic (*Tempest* 5.1.54), the rod that Merlin uses to quell his enemies in *The Birth of Merlin*.

Given the expectations of a context where conjuring and witchcraft have been so important, it astonishes me that no one has suggested that the staff Macbeth calls for at 5.3.48 is a magic staff. Editors call it "either a weapon or a staff of office" (Brooke). How does one identify it as either from its appearance? There would be no problem identifying a magic staff *from its association with a wizard's cloak*—and that is just what Beerbohm Tree (in 1911) had Hecate's spirits put on Macbeth at the end of the necromancy scene, where the spirits come to restore his confidence.[15] We have seen the precedent for this. Faustus, too, after his commerce with the devil, feels weak and regretful—so the devils dance for him and give him rich apparel, the wizard's garb that replaces his clerical garb. I suggest that Hecate's spirits do the same for Macbeth. The stage direction was lost at the same time Hecate's expanded song was added to the play (to be cued in short form by the Folio).

When Macbeth comes to the necromancy, he asks the witches to conjure for him in his own witch-speech. But he is, at this stage, still an initiate brought to his first conjuring—like the Duchess of Gloucester in *II Henry VI*. After his participation, he is both privileged and damned, given powers that will self-destruct. Just before his next appearance, before the only two scenes where he can wear the mantle, we hear Angus compare his title to "a giant's robe / Upon a dwarfed thief" (5.2.21–22).

The robe would look like a king's robe. Monarchs had emblems on their apparel—like the zodiacal signs and mystical symbols on Elizabeth's garment in the Rainbow Portrait, painted circa 1603, or the wondrous cloak of mirrors put on Edward III.[16] The Titania (Elizabeth) whose court is contrasted with Rome's in Dekker's *Whore* has a "faery" court where symbols of "good" magic and providential order are contrasted with the trappings of the Beast's kingdom.

The magic cloak of Macbeth the conjurer may even help clear up a textual dispute. At 5.3.21, the Folio has Macbeth say, "This push / Will cheere me ever, or dis-eate me now." Editors regularly alter "cheere" to "chair," so it will match "dis-seat." But the push is Macbeth's, not a challenger's—as it should be if a push, by *failing*, lets him *keep* his chair. He is not *taking* it. If we keep the text, with his garment in mind, it would remind us of the reason he was given it by Hecate (4.1.127):

> Come, sisters, cheer we up his sprites!

What becomes, then, of the emphatically syllabified "dis-eate," a non-word? Many since Rowe have accepted the Second Folio's "dis-ease." Compare Chapman's "dis-ease" when he had Mercury *take away* the ease of sleep:

> Then up his rod went, with which he declin'd
> The eyes of any waker when he pleas'd,
> And any sleeper, when he wish'd, dis-eased.[17]

Macbeth's loss will take away the cheering ease the witches brought him.

The long business with the armor reflects Macbeth's reluctance to surrender his robe and staff. He asks for armor, then says instead, "Give me my staff." There are two possibilities in what follows. Either he says "Pull't off, I say" of his cloak—like Prospero's "Pluck my magic garment from me"—and then says "bring it after me" of the cloak. Or he begins to arm, stops, and says, "Bring the *armor* after me."

I prefer the second choice. It takes Macbeth into a third scene wearing his cloak. He disrobes in the gathering doubts that follow on reports of his wife's death—perhaps during the "Tomorrow and tomorrow" speech. He becomes only a man again, like Prospero without his wand, like Faustus and Alexander trying to repent. Then he calls up his manic courage and arms with a desperate glee (5.5.51): "At least we'll die with harness on our back."

The "Tomorrow and tomorrow" speech (5.5.19–28) is a confession that Macbeth has been all too successful in canceling time. He has turned it into a meaningless succession of sameness. If conjuring is an attempt to master time and space by stepping outside both, to exert a power over the universe, this is a speech of supreme powerlessness.[18] Its weary cadence seems to be an inversion of the message of Psalm 19 (verses 2 and 4):

> Day unto day uttreth the same
> > And night unto night teacheth knowledge. . . .
> Their line is gone forth through all the earth,
> > And their words unto the ends of the world.[19]

Yet Macbeth still clings to belief in his own preternatural immunities. He has a pledge on the future, what he called "a bond of fate" (4.1.84). Two impossibilities protect him—no man born of woman can kill him, and Birnam Wood must walk. But the fated end of contracting with the devil is to see that the contract was a trick. The assurance turns into a trap. As the Gunpowder Plotters saw their own scheme recoil upon them (those who dug the pit falling into it), so Macbeth finds that there was a meaning to the pledges that he did not grasp.

In both cases, it is a meaning traditional to witchcraft. Making woods move is a part of the witches' regular impossibilities (*adynata*). Even Macbeth hinted at this in his conjuring speech. Classical witches regularly boast *Et silvas moveo*. Macbeth should have suspected such portents, however contrived. He had said himself, "Stones have been known to move and trees to speak" (3.4.122).

The other portent is also traditional with witches. They especially prize unbaptized infants for creating spells. They steal them from cribs or ditches where they die. They even rip them from pregnant corpses, as Lucan said in the passage used by Marston for the necromancy scene in *Sophonisba*.

> *Volnere sic ventris, non qua natura vocabat,*
> *Extrahitur partus, calidis ponendus in aris.*[20]
> By a stab to the womb, in a way nature never indicated,
> The child is torn out to be offered on the flaming altar.

This is a passage Ben Jonson cited in his notes to *The Masque of Queens*.[21]

The witches formed their riddles in ways that could turn backwards on their victim. When the portents come true, however, it is not by some preternatural intrusion into the order of nature. The walking wood and man not born are *fake* miracles, as it were—natural events masquerading in odd language. The witches are equivocators in the most thoroughgoing way. Like the Jesuits, they use words that are true at some level but not in the way that their victim could understand. They "keep the word of promise to our ear / And break it to our hope" (5.8.21–22). It is what Banquo had predicted on the heath (1.3.123–26):

> And oftentimes, to win us to our harm,
> The instruments of Darkness tell us truths,
> Win us with honest trifles, to betray's
> In deepest consequence.

The unnatural thing is not Birnam Wood's moving or Macduff's non-birth birth, but the unnatural (Jesuitical) language of the witches, the destruction of reality in *words* misused. No wonder Macbeth says, when the wood moves, "I pale in resolution, and begin / To doubt th' equivocation of the fiend" (5.5.41–42).[22]

But Macbeth fights on, relying on the other portent, which is harder to fulfill in any conceivable natural sense. He can still boast to Macduff, "I bear a charmed life." The charm is the magic spell woven around him by the witches in the necromancy scene. The marking off of "charmed" ground has occurred many times in the play—on the heath as the witches circled Macbeth, in "hell" as the Porter circled his imagined Jesuit, in the necromancy scene, in the fake spell cast by Malcolm on Macduff. The actual geometry of magic figures on the ground is important to scenes like those of Faustus's and Pope Alexander's conjuring or in the marked arena of Faustus's witchcraft illustrated in the 1620 Quarto (see Frontispiece). We should suppose that the charmed circle is a spot still definite on the stage as Macbeth, stripped of followers, retreats to his last redoubt of magic. Imagine him taking up that position as he prepares to kill Siward. His circle has become the ambit of a bear staked for baiting (5.7.1–2):

> They have tied me to a stake. I cannot fly
> But bearlike I must fight the course.

The bear is circumscribed, and his circle can contract if the chain winds around the pole as he turns and backs away from baiting dogs; but Macbeth still sees it as a circle of power, and he kills young Siward with fiendish energy. The charges of diabolic power are made both by Siward and, especially, by Macduff: "Turn, hellhound!" (5.8.3). The bravery of young Siward and of Macduff cannot properly be gauged unless we take seriously the hellish aspect of Macbeth's power. These men are in the position of desperate pursuers who must "take on" a vampire in Dracula movies. Macduff acts like an exorcist (5.8.13–15):

> Despair thy charm!
> And let the Angel whom thou still hast serv'd
> Tell thee . . .

Macduff forces Macbeth out of his charmed circle—which explains the odd Folio direction: *Exeunt fighting. Alarums. Enter fighting, and Macbeth slain.* This breaks Poel's Rule against actors' exiting and immediately re-entering. It has been plausibly suggested that Macbeth is forced out on the lower stage and reappears on the upper level, where the business of beheading him after he falls can more easily be feigned. The retreat to higher inner levels of a castle was a familiar concept to the audience—as if the bear's ambit were narrowing and narrowing around his stake—and the head could be brandished from the balcony as from battlements (Welles filmed it that way). The spell is broken, the circle shattered. "The time is free."

conclusion

*The Test of
Performance*

D o I make *Macbeth* too weird? I anticipate objectors, saying: "How are performers to make sense of so much
topical allusion, time-bound politics, and all-permeating
magic—all the diablerie, conjuring, and circles?" Grant the objection.
To say *Macbeth* will not work on the modern stage is not, of itself, to
invalidate the interpretation I offer, based as that is on Jacobean
concerns, stage fashions, and language.

But is it true that the political-theological aspects of the play are
impossible to deal with on the modern stage? It is not as though
Macbeth, played without these concerns, has been a stage success. The
modern record of the play has been notoriously bad. Perhaps that is
because directors have shied too energetically *away* from the text's
clear indication of a theological politics at work.

The witches are an embarrassment to many producers. Not only is
Hecate cut from the play; some have even cut the witches' opening
scene. The witches are to be marginalized, made symbols, reduced to
Coleridge's "atmosphere." Is this, just as theater, an efficient pro-

cedure? The popularity of vampire books and movies shows that stories dealing with Dark Forces can work with a general audience. If the witches are there, and prominent, in the first half of the play, whatever sinister vitality they bring to the action is drained away when the second half is deprived of their influence.

What we get in many cases is a supernatural first part of the play followed by a secular second part. Why has no one connected this with the general verdict that modern productions are anticlimactic? The poor bloodless Malcolm of modern stagings cannot attain the status of a man defying cosmic evil. The guilt of Lady Macbeth lacks the Faustian aspect of one who has singed her hands in hell. And, since taking away the theology in the time of the Gunpowder Plot means taking away the politics, the fate of Scotland is no longer a matter of urgency in the final scene. The story is reduced to that of a murderer getting his just penalty, in place of a struggle for the soul of a nation. We are sometimes, it is said, given a Hamlet Without the Prince. We almost always get a Macbeth Without the Prince.

I have argued that the witches represent a diabolic element that is just as present in the second half of the play as in the first—in Malcolm's reverse spell and benign equivocation, in Macbeth's conjurer's confidence over his bond with hell, in Lady Macbeth's sense that she has become a spiritual (though not a legal) witch.

Can this be made to work on the modern stage? The odds seem to me good. The modern performances that have come closest to success were based on intuitions close to some of the interpretations offered here. Olivier began as a man curious to dabble in an experience of evil and ended with the monstrous energies he drew from this perversion of his own nature. Orson Welles's "voodoo Macbeth" adopted a coherent spiritual system from Haiti, integrating the politics and the theology of the play. Followers of Ian Kott have spread a kind of indiscriminate nihilism over many of Shakespeare's plays—which could better be applied to the diabolism of *Macbeth*. Trevor Nunn's 1976 production was ritualized throughout, played in a circle, using a hieratic robe as the main stage prop, doubling actors to bring out the "chimings" of acts performed in an infectious atmosphere of evil.

All these were steps, small or large, toward the kind of reintegrated *Macbeth* I argue for, one that does not fall into separate parts, into warring superstitious and secular components—one that can be truly cursed by the witches and will *therefore* escape the theatrical curse on "the Scottish play."

Appendix I

Date of the Play

Gary Taylor, the editor of the Oxford Works of Shakespeare, wrote in 1993, "Macbeth was almost certainly composed in the summer of 1606."[1] That certitude is surprising, since the only text we have of *Macbeth* is in the 1623 Folio and the only external evidence of its performance is Simon Forman's attendance at one in 1611. But 1606 is the date most editors accept confidently (e.g., Kenneth Muir in the 1984 revision of his Arden edition) or tentatively (e.g., Nicholas Brooke in his 1990 Oxford commentary).

Why this consensus? It depends on a structure of probabilities, none strong enough in itself to determine the matter, but cumulatively persuasive. There are four kinds of evidence normally adduced, and I would add a fifth.

1. Stylistic criteria. "The metrical test and the colloquialism-inverse test both place *Macbeth* after *Lear* and *Timon* but before *Antony*. Oras's pause tests also place it after *Lear* but before *Antony*. The rareword test links it most closely to the earlier tragedies *Hamlet* and *Troilus*, and to *Lear*."[2] All these aspects of the language indicate that there were performances earlier than the one Forman saw in 1611, and they sit most easily in the period when *Lear* and *Antony* were written—*Lear* surely in 1606 and *Antony* probably in 1606–07.

2. Topical references in the play. The treatment of equivocation links the play to Henry Garnet's famous trial and execution as an equivocator in March–May, 1606. The reference to troubles for the ship *Tiger* (1.3.7ff) is taken to refer to a famously disastrous voyage that ended on June 27, 1606.[3] A third event that has not so far been used for the dating of the play is the reference to the English tailor and his "goose" at 2.3.13–15, which H. L. Rogers plausibly relates to an investigation of a tailor connected with Garnet, one that began in November, 1606.[4]

3. Other authors' references to the play. Several have been cited, but only one carries real conviction, Beaumont's at *The Knight of the Burning Pestle* 5.1.22–28.[5] This play is best dated to 1607–08.[6]

4. The use of Plutarch at *Macbeth* 3.1.55 resembles use of the same source at *Antony* 2.3.16–20 and suggests to some that the plays were worked on simultaneously or in close succession. This would confirm the linguistic links with *Antony* (and therefore with *Lear*).

The evidence above is listed in decreasing order of weightiness. But a fifth consideration deserves to be ranked near the first item in its suasive force.

5. The constellation of elements shared with other plays referring to the Gunpowder Plot—with Marston's *Sophonisba*, Dekker's *The Whore of Babylon*, and Barnes's *The Devil's Charter*—would make *Macbeth* contemporary with them, in 1606 or 1607. All these plays share with *Macbeth* the following aspects: witches, a necromancy scene, regicide attempted or completed, references to equivocation, scenes that test loyalty by use of deceptive language, and a character who sees through plots—along with a vocabulary closely connected to the Plot in its immediate aftermath (words like *train, blow, vault*) and an ironic recoil of the Plot upon the Plotters (who fall into the pit they dug).

This configuration of shared elements closely links *Macbeth* to the other Gunpowder plays, according to the argument of this book. The date that others have adopted I treat as an hypothesis that is confirmed not only by association with Marston, Dekker, and Barnes, but with other literature dealing with the Plot (speeches by the King and his churchmen, poems like *The Devil of the Vault* and *The Jesuits' Miracles*).

If a date in 1606–07 is accepted, can the time of earliest performance be even more narrowly pinned down? H. N. Paul thought so, when he argued for a performance in honor of King Christian of Denmark's visit to Hampton Court. Paul claims the play was first seen at Hampton Court on August 6, 1606. It is true that there were celebrations for Christian, but that king, who could speak no English, was no doubt more intrigued by the ambitious bearbaiting schedule.⁷ Paul sees *Macbeth* as a tissue of specific references to James, Christian, and their royal relationship. Few of these ingenious references have convinced later scholars, and Paul underestimates the preparation time Shakespeare would have had for the unpredictable scheduling of the kings' peregrinations.⁸

Leeds Barroll argues that *Macbeth* could not have been put on in London's public theaters after June of 1606, when the theaters were closed by the plague.⁹ This leaves little time for immediate production after Garnet's execution (May 1). H. L. Rogers's suggestion that the "English tailor" reference follows the investigation of Garnet's straw, on November 25, would push *Macbeth* into the performing season that began at court on December 26. This period included a heavy court celebration of the Twelve Days of Christmas, beginning with the acting of *King Lear* on December 26 and extending as far as the acting of Barnes's *The Devil's Charter* on Candlemas (February 2). Since it has also been argued that *Antony and Cleopatra* was performed in this season, some hesitate to shove *Macbeth* into such a busy time for the king's troupe.[10] But the use of common stage effects (e.g., the necromancy scenes in *Macbeth* and *The Devil's Charter*), the concentration of witch-enchantress roles for an outstanding boy actor (Lady Macbeth—Lucretia Borgia—Cleopatra), and the stylistic tests binding *Lear-Macbeth-Antony* in the closest relationship, all argue for performance within a narrow time span.

Some doubt that Shakespeare could compose three such masterpieces as *Lear* and *Macbeth* and *Antony* in a single year. But Barroll has noted that Shakespeare wrote in productive bursts.[11] The closing of the theaters would give him time to write. Getting the works licensed and the parts written out could be done in the plague season, as could the actors' training of apprentices, memorization of parts, and necessary rehearsals (mainly of songs, dances, and fights). Burbage's troupe had been embarrassed when, for whatever reason, it ran short of new plays in the 1604–05 Christmas season.[12] The players more than made up for that in the 1606–07 Christmas season, when they presented nine plays.

Though an original *Macbeth* was probably performed in that 1606–07 Christmas season, the Folio text does not give us that original. The casting explosion that occurs when Hecate enters with three more witches, a familiar spirit, and a chorus reflects conditions different from those evident in the rest of the play. It points to indoor performance with access to a larger number of boy actors (including singers and dancers) and resources for greater spectacle (including costumes as well as flying machinery).

It is generally accepted that these additions occurred at some revival of *Macbeth* before the troupe published the 1623 Folio. Other changes could have been made in the play at the same time. Some attribute its brevity to the revision, since *Macbeth* is the shortest tragedy and the third shortest play.[13] But cutting back on the play when new resources became available is not a likely project.[14]

Attempts to date the revision have centered on three arguments:

1. The masque elements of the revised *Macbeth* may reflect Ben Jonson's pageant of witches in *The Masque of Queens,* performed at Whitehall on February 2, 1609. Some have even suggested that the extra costumes called for by the addition of Hecate's retinue could have been supplied from Jonson's production.[15] But see the next argument against dating the revision prior to 1610.

2. Simon Forman may have seen a revised version of the play at the Globe on April 20, 1611. Nicholas Brooke takes this view. But a public theater does not comport with the private conditions reflected in the new Hecate scenes. Nor does Forman even mention Hecate. He probably saw a repeat performance of the original version. Admittedly, the troupe could have played the original version in the Globe *after* having put on an altered version at court or in a private mansion. But that presents licensing problems. The censor normally authorized only one playing version of a drama.[16]

3. The principal attempt to date the revision comes from its supposed relation to Middleton's *The Witch,* a play lost at the time of Davenant's Restoration version of *Macbeth,* which incorporated songs from *The Witch.* The assumption is that Davenant had access to song texts (cued but not reproduced at Folio *Macbeth* 3.4 and 4.1) in papers descended from the company. When a copy of Middleton's play was finally printed in 1778, it had Middleton's prefixed comment that the play had failed. It was assumed that when the play did not work, the songs were salvaged from it for use in *Macbeth.* This thesis was especially appealing to those who think the Hecate scenes are entirely

out of place in *Macbeth*, an intrusion that shows the artistic insensibility of Shakespeare's troupe—first, in making the switch, and then in printing this "defaced" version of the play. I have discussed this aesthetic judgment in Chapter Two.

Here we are concerned with dates. *Macbeth*'s relation to *The Witch* (whatever that may be) cannot help date *Macbeth*'s revision if *The Witch* cannot itself be dated. Some relate it to Jonson's *The Masque of Queens* (1609), others to the aftermath of Frances Howard's divorce from the Earl of Essex (1615). Students of the play's relation to that divorce argue that it must *precede* the divorce trial, and reflect rumors about the "bewitched" marriage circulating around 1613—or the middle point in the range of six years or so suggested for the play's composition.[17] The usefulness of *The Witch* for dating purposes also depends on the assumption that *The Witch* precedes *Macbeth*'s revision, since its "flop" frees up the songs for other use. But Anne Lancashire has successfully challenged the myth of a "flop."[18]

A precise date for *Macbeth*'s revision is currently impossible. Most presume it was accomplished by 1613, when Shakespeare was still working with the troupe of which he remained a shareholder. So his approval of the result is likely, even if Middleton is the composer of Hecate's scenes. The two men had collaborated on *Timon* as early as 1605–06.

Even if the revision occurred after 1613, the troupe clearly thought it an appropriate replacement for whatever original stood in its place (we cannot assume the scenes are simply added, without removing earlier passages, probably of Hecate without attendants).[19] The thesis that the Hecate scenes are a crude theatrical violation of Shakespeare's play was formulated when the playwright was treated as a lone romantic genius, at odds with his own colleagues and resisting concessions to "the groundlings." That misconceives the collaborative nature of his theater company. We are not in a position to consider ourselves superior to Burbage and his fellows in carrying out the intentions of the original *Macbeth*, refracted to us only in the text the King's Men used and kept and published. (This does *not* mean that the songs cued in the Folio were *exactly* those from *The Witch*. The cat-familiar is out of place in *Macbeth*. All the cues tell us is that *some* version of the songs was included. The songs Davenant read were separated from the Folio.)

Appendix II
Text of the Play

I cite Shakespeare's plays by the line numbers in *The Riverside Shakespeare* (Houghton Mifflin Company, 1974), since Marvin Spevack's *Harvard Concordance to Shakespeare* (1973) is keyed to that text. But aside from line numbers, I use, eclectically, other editions (principally Arden and Oxford) for specific plays, while modernizing orthography.

If we except Hecate's songs, the only source of *Macbeth's* text is the 1623 Folio. Hecate's song-scenes have been thoroughly edited only by Nicholas Brooke in his 1990 Oxford edition of the play. I cite his lineation for those scenes. For the rest of the play, while citing lines by the Riverside system, I work directly from the Folio in Charlton Hinman's Norton Facsimile (1968), which conflates the Folger Folios. Changes from that text (other than modernization of orthography) are of three kinds.

I accept some common editorial emendations. For instance:

1.2.13 Steevens gallowglasses for F Gallowgrosses

1.2.26 Pope break, after F Thunders

1.3.39 Pope Forres, for F Soris

1.6.4 Rowe martlet, for F Barlet

1.6.5 Theobald mansionry, for F Mansonry

1.6.9 Rowe most, for F must

2.1.56 Capell sure, for F sowre

2.1.57 Rowe way they, for F they may

4.1.59 Theobald germens for F Germaine

4.3.34 Hanmer affeer'd for F affear'd

5.3.21 Rowe dis-ease (after F2) for F dis-eate

In some places I retain the F reading where modern editions often alter it:

1.2.14 F Quarry, not Johnson quarrel

1.3.97 F Tale, not Rowe hail

1.3.98 F Can, not Rowe Came

1.7.6 F Schoole, not Theobald shoal

3.2.13 F scorch'd ("slashed"), not Theobald scotched

4.3.235 F time, not Rowe tune

In a few cases, with proper trepidation, I suggest new readings:

1.2.61 Colme-his (possessive case) for F Colmes

1.3.96 affeer'd for F afeard

1.7.6 rank for F Banke

2.1.55 sights for F sides

5.2.27 med'c'ner for F Med'cine

5.5.41 pale for F pull

My reasons for these readings can be found by using the line-index to *Macbeth*. I append two further notes on the text:

1. *The Weyard Sisters.* F's Compositor A set *weyward*, Compositor B *weyard*. Most editors think this is just a way of indicating that Holinshed's *weird* is to be pronounced dissyllabically. (Of course, the settings also indicate vowel sound—e as in *grey*, not as in *week*.) Shakespeare never uses *weird*, but often uses *wayward*. He may have been etymologizing weird as (among other things) wayward. The exotic word would fit the odd witches, who are out of nature's way— the meaning Wycliffe gave to *wayward* in translating things that departed from the biblical path of righteousness: a wayward (damned) generation, waywardness as wickedness, a wayward (perverse) judgment, a wayward (uncontrolled) mouth or eye.[1] Shakespeare uses wayward, meaning intractable, mainly of children (and especially of Cupid) or of diseases.[2] Thomas Heywood (or Richard Brome) understood the witches to be "Scottish Wayward Sisters" (*The Witches of Lancashire*, line 447). Of the Compositors' two versions of the phrase, the *lectio difficilior* is B's (A's weyward could be a mere spelling variant of wayward); so I think it should stand as an exotic form Shakespeare thought of as connecting his source in Holinshed with a suggestion of waywardness. The sisters are outside the course, or way, of nature. Unnatural, in Wycliffe's sense.

2. *Strange images of death* (1.3.97). Why, if Macbeth so calmly inflicts death, is the king amazed that he is "nothing afear'd" of death? Empson has Duncan, who "must have known a great deal about Macbeth's habit of mind, anticipate Macbeth's later fear of death's

image [Banquo's ghost]." But this contradicts what we know of Duncan's inability to construe others' minds in their faces.[3]

The controlling fact of the passage is the king's perception. He is first silenced between wonder and praise. Then he "views" the day (from afar) and gets reports of the dead—their "images" that come from the scene thicker than can be counted ("told"), and that bear Macbeth's praises. Why is Macbeth "nothing afear'd"? The word may be "affeer'd," as at line 4.3.34 of this play. Macbeth is not fined for this busy coinage of death's images—he is exempt from the Norweyans' power to prohibit his ghastly commerce.

Macbeth makes images of death as men *coin* "heaven's image" in bastards at *Measure for Measure* 2.4.45, or as Falstaff calls dead bodies "counterfeit" men at *I Henry IV* 5.4. 115–17. "Tale" as the *count* goes with this imagery of coining/counterfeiting (a favorite with Shakespeare). Macbeth, unfined, strikes off his images as fast as tale can bear report, just as Autolycus "sings several tunes faster than you'll tell money" (*Winter's Tale* 4.4.183–84).[4] Thus, "tale / Can" of F can be retained, but with punctuation that shows the reports (images) are as thick as *counting* can (and each post does) bear praises. The passage, with "affeer'd for "afear'd," would then be punctuated:

> The king hath happily receiv'd, Macbeth,
> The news of thy success, and when he reads
> Thy personal venture in the rebels' fight,
> His wonders and praises do contend
> Which should be thine or his, silenc'd with that.
> In viewing o'er the rest o' th' selfsame day,
> He finds thee in the stout Norweyan ranks
> Nothing affeer'd of what thyself doth make,

> Strange images of death, as thick as tale
> Can—post with post, and every one did—bear
> Thy praises in his kingdom's great defense
> And pour'd them down before him.

There is nothing certain about these suggestions; and my book's principal argument—about the ties between *Macbeth* and other Gunpowder plays—does not depend on any of them. I offer them only where I cannot make sense of the accepted text (itself a product of emendation in most of these places). In some cases the text may be too corrupt for recovery.

Key to Brief Citations

Brooke   *The Tragedy of Macbeth*, edited by Nicholas Brooke (The Oxford Shakespeare, 1990).

Daemonologie   James VI of Scotland, *Daemonologie*, in *Minor Prose Works of James VI and I*, edited by James Craigie (Scottish Text Society, 1982).

The Devil's Charter   Barnabe Barnes, *The Devil's Charter*, edited by Jim C. Pogue (Garland Publishing, 1980).

Doctor Faustus   Christopher Marlowe, *Doctor Faustus*, edited by David Bevington and Eric Rasmussen (Manchester University Press, 1993).

Muir   *Macbeth*, edited by Kenneth Muir, new edition, 1984 (The Arden Edition, Methuen).

Rosenberg   Marvin Rosenberg, *The Masks of Macbeth* (University of Delaware Press, 1978).

Sophonisba   John Marston, *The Wonder of Women, or The Tragedy of Sophonisba*, edited by Peter Corbin and Douglas Sedge, in *Three Jacobean Witch-craft Plays* (Manchester University Press, 1986).

STC	*A Short-Title Catalogue of Books Printed in England, Scotland, & Ireland, and of Books, Printed Abroad, 1475–1640.*
Variorum	*Macbeth, A New Variorum Edition,* edited by Horace Howard Furness Jr., Fifth Edition (J. B. Lippincott & Company, 1873).
The Whore of Babylon	Thomas Dekker, *The Whore of Babylon,* edited by Fredson Bowers, *Dramatic Works of Thomas Dekker,* Vol. 2 (Cambridge University Press, 1955).
The Witch	Thomas Middleton, *A Tragicomedy Called the Witch,* edited by Peter Corbin and Douglas Sedge, in *Three Jacobean Witchcraft Plays* (Manchester University Press, 1986).
The Witch of Edmonton	William Rowley, Thomas Dekker, John Ford, *The Witch of Edmonton,* edited by Peter Corbin and Douglas Sedge, in *Three Jacobean Witchcraft Plays* (Manchester University Press, 1986).

Notes

Introduction

1. "Originally invited to direct *Macbeth*, [Peter] Brook had refused—surprisingly, for so austerely cerebral a man—because of the Scottish play's reputation for ill-luck." Anthony Holden, *Laurence Olivier* (Atheneum, 1988), 295. Judi Dench, after an experience with a "cursed" production in South Africa, resolved never to play Lady Macbeth again—though in time she was persuaded to relent. See her interview with Gareth Lloyd Evans in *Shakespeare Survey* 17 (1974): 141.

2. See, for instance, Richard Huggett, *The Curse of Macbeth and Other Theatrical Superstitions* (Picton Publishing, 1981), 133–213.

3. Ibid., 153–54.

4. Bernice W. Kliman, *Shakespeare in Performance: "Macbeth"* (Manchester University Press, 1992), 54.

5. Elisabeth Nielsen, *"Macbeth:* The Nemesis of the Post-Shakespearian Actor," *Shakespeare Quarterly* 16 (1965): 193. She continues: "Famous men have played the role, but they have gained their fame elsewhere first."

6. Kenneth Tynan, *A View of the English Stage, 1944–1963* (Davis-Poynter, 1975), 156.

7. Kliman, op, cit., 40, on the critical consensus about Glen Byam Shaw's production with Olivier and Vivien Leigh in the lead parts.

8. The Macbeth in Trevor Nunn's 1979 TV production (Ian McKellen) had a seizure and foamed at the mouth on the ghost's second appearance. Charles Kean and Christopher Plummer clung to the actress playing Lady Macbeth like children with their mother. See Rosenberg, 449.

Notes

9. For the blocking and performing of these scenes, see the well-illustrated *"Macbeth" Onstage: An Annotated Facsimile of Glen Byam Shaw's 1955 Promptbook*, edited by Michael Mullin (University of Missouri Press, 1976), 114–53.

10. "At 'Lay on, Macduff,' Olivier seemed inexplicably to grow in height: he was seen as a lion turning gradually at bay." Rosenberg, 647.

11. Tynan, op, cit., 156, on the play's problem as normally performed:

> Instead of growing as the play proceeds, the hero shrinks; complex and many-leveled to begin with, he ends up a cornered thug, lacking even a death scene with which to regain his lost stature [a lack David Garrick repaired by writing in his own death scene]. Most Macbeths, mindful of this, set off their big guns as soon as possible, and have usually shot their bolt by the time the dagger speech is out. The marvel of Sir Laurence's reading is that it reverses this procedure, turning the play inside out, and makes it (for the first time I can remember) a thing of mounting, not waning, excitement.

Welles was so convinced that the play fell into two distinct parts that he claimed no Macbeth "can play the first *and* second half. An actor who can do one can't do the other. . . . I've never seen that problem successfully bridged. Certainly, I didn't." Orson Welles and Peter Bogdanovich, *This Is Orson Welles* (Harper Collins, 1992), 216–17.

12. David Rosen and Andrew Porter, *Verdi's "Macbeth." A Sourcebook* (W. W. Norton, 1984), 4–5. Verdi conceived the opera with only two lead singers after he heard that no important tenor was available.

13. Ibid., 110. Lady Macbeth's voice should be muffled (*suffocata*), according to the composer (p. 67).

14. The scenery of Welles's film is unlocalized and non-specific, reflecting the lack of an exterior objective order against which Macbeth can test himself. "The spatial substance, in some affinitive way, takes on the involuntary biochemistry of Macbeth. Its cavernous walls exude drops of moisture just as Macbeth's skin glistens with the torrid sweat of panic." Anthony Davies, *Filming Shakespeare's Plays* (Cambridge University Press, 1988), 89. André Bazin said the union of Macbeth's mind and the shapeless mud of the outer world was signaled in the film's early scene, where the witches make a voodoo-doll of Macbeth: *Orson Welles: A Critical View*, translated by Jonathan Rosenbaum (Harper & Row, 1978), 101.

15. D. J. Snider, quoted in Variorum, 408. Cf. H. Ulrici, at p. 435:

They are the fearful echo which the natural and spiritual world gives back to the evil which sounds forth from within the human breast itself . . . . Their flattering promises do but represent the cunning self-deception which nestles within the guilty bosom.

16. Kliman, op. cit., 41: "Several critics who attended the opening night, 7 June 1955, blasted it for Macbeth's quiet, unheroic beginning." And p. 48: "The courted risk" refers to the choice of hoarding Macbeth's reserves for the last act.

17. For the play's date, see Appendix One.

18. What I am calling Gunpowder plays correspond to the group David Bevington considered together as Armada plays. The outpouring of literature and official propaganda in the aftermath of the Armada invasion was the equivalent, in Elizabeth's time, of the Gunpowder literature in James's reign. We would expect this huge effort to be reflected in the theater, and our expectation is fulfilled. See Bevington, *Tudor Drama and Politics* (Harvard University Press, 1968), chap. 14, "War Fever."

One · Gunpowder

1. See J. R. Hale, "Gunpowder and the Renaissance," *Renaissance War Studies* (Hambledon Press, 1983), 389–420.

2. Coke referred, at the Plotters' trial, to the murder by a monk of the French king Henry III in 1589 (W. J. Adams, *The Gunpowder Treason* (London, 1851), 108). This atrocity was often denounced, as in Marlowe's *The Massacre at Paris*, Scene 23. Lacey Baldwin Smith instructs me that the Catholic menace was far greater in England (based on sheer numbers) than any communist menace America experienced.

3. For Catholic disagreement on how to deal with the rapid religious changes in England, see especially Peter Holmes, *Resistance and Compromise: The Political Thought of the Elizabethan Jesuits* (Cambridge University Press, 1982). Also useful are: Thomas H. Clancy, S. J., *Papist Pamphleteers: The Allen-Persons Party and the Political Thought of the Counter-Reformation in England, 1572–1615* (Loyola University Press, 1964); Eliot Rose, *Cases of Conscience: Alternatives Open to Recusants and Puritans Under Elizabeth I and James I* (Cambridge University Press, 1975); Adrian Morey, *The Catholic Subjects of Elizabeth I* (George Allen & Unwin, 1978); Kenneth L. Campbell,

The Intellectual Struggle of the English Papists in the Seventeenth Century (Edwin Mellen Press, 1986).

4. Since these governments orchestrated reaction in a time of crisis, suspicion that the official version was invented as well as emphasized was bound to arise. In President Roosevelt's case it was alleged that he had stage-managed the nation into war, accepting the blow to Pearl Harbor as the price of mobilizing the nation. In President Johnson's case, it was alleged that the Warren Commission was established to cover up a conspiracy involving parts of the government itself. In King James's case, it was alleged that the government provoked the Plot, or at least encouraged it, to discredit the Jesuits. I do not believe any of these skeptical theories, which were brought on by governmental efforts to control emotion in a crisis. For a recent statement of the view that the Gunpowder Treason was created by *agents provocateurs*, see Francis Edwards, S. J., "Still Investigating Gunpowder Plot," *Recusant History* 21 (May 1993): 305–46.

5. See *The Apocalypse in English Renaissance Thought and Literature*, edited by C. A. Patrides and Joseph Wittreich (Cornell University Press, 1984); and Katherine R. Firth, *The Apocalyptic Tradition in Reformation Britain, 1530–1645* (Oxford University Press, 1979).

6. A similar relaxation had occurred after the Armada invasion. See Virginia Crocheron Gildersleeve, *Government Regulations of the Elizabethan Drama* (Columbia University Press, 1908), 92.

7. See Joel Hurstfield, "Gunpowder Plot and the Politics of Dissent," *Early Stuart Studies*, edited by H. S. Reinmuth (University of Minnesota Press, 1970).

8. For James's controversy with Bellarmino, see the introduction by Charles Howard McIlwain to *The Political Works of James I* (Harvard University Press, 1918). For Lancelot Andrewes's contribution to the controversy, see his *Responsio ad Apologiam Cardinalis Bellarmini*. Andrewes, *Works* (Oxford University Press, 1851), Vol. 7.

9. *The Devil of the Vault* (1606; STC 12568).

10. James, "Speech in the Parliament House," McIlwain, op. cit., 281–83.

11. Ibid., 289.

12. Ibid., 283–84.

13. Ibid., 285.

14. Ibid., 284, citing Psalm 9.15.

15. William Barlow, Lord Bishop of Rochester, Sermon of November 1606 at Paul's Cross (STC 1455). The enduring imagery in which the Plot was conceived

can be gauged from Milton's 1626 poem on the Plot, which takes up Barlow's picture of James blown to heaven like the charioted Elias: *In Proditionem Bombardicam*, lines 5–10.

16. Compare *The Devil of the Vault:*

> So pitiless powder did conspire
> Their never-ending end.

17. Sir John Hayward, a knowledgeable court observer, said the King was hidden in Westminster Hall. See Mark Nicholls, *Investigating Gunpowder Plot* (Manchester University Press, 1991), 52. Coke, in any case, knew the King's great interest in his prosecution, and composed with that in mind.

18. Coke's speeches were printed in *A True and Perfect Relation of the Whole Proceedings Against the Late most Barbarous Traitors, Garnet a Jesuit and His Confederates* (1606; STC 11618–19), reprinted frequently under different titles. I use the 1851 London edition edited by W. J. Adams, under the title *The Gunpowder Treason*, p. 111.

19. Ibid., 121–22: "Note that gunpowder was the invention of a friar [Bacon], one of that Romish rabble."

20. Ibid.

21. Ibid., 116. For diabolic confusion—the anti-rule of the kingdom of disorder —see note 43 below.

22. Ibid., 162.

23. For words as natural, not artificial, bearers of meaning in Shakespeare's time, see Anne Barton, *The Names of Comedy* (University of Toronto Press, 1990), 3–15; and Gary Tomlinson, *Music in Renaissance Magic* (University of Chicago Press, 1993), 115–21.

24. Thomas Dekker, *The Double P: A Papist in Arms Bearing Ten Several Shields, Encountered by the Protestant* (1606; STC 6498).

25. Adams, op. cit., 121.

26. Ibid., 167.

27. Lancelot Andrewes, "A Sermon Preached Before the King's Majesty at Whitehall," Andrewes, *Works*, 4: 207.

28. Ibid., 212. The planned horrors of the Plot did not lose their fascination for Andrewes. Ten years later he could still call up the vision of

> men tumbling in their own blood, here and there, in the streets . . . men torn
> in sunder, heads from shoulders, arms from legs, both from the body; quarters

and half-quarters flying about; the brains fly one way, the bowels another; blood spilt like water in the river, in the fields, in every corner of the streets [ibid., 397].

This is another case of what the Plotters plotted backfiring on them, since they were executed by hanging, drawing and quartering, their blood emptied out, heads separated from bodies, quarters dismantled. As Andrewes put it in his first Powder Sermon, "their quarters stand now in pieces, as they meant ours should" (p. 217). See Coke's speech for the prosecution (Adams, op. cit., 124). The Bishop of Rochester, too, dwelt on the Plotters' effort to "discerp [rip] and tear parcel-meal the bodies." Compare the popular poem, *The Devil of the Vault:* "Piecemeal to rive the Parliament."

29. Andrewes, op. cit., 4: 217.

30. *The Jesuits' Miracles* (1606; STC 20340).

31. The contract with the devil could be read two ways, so the Pope finds he has been cheated of seven years when he has to give up his soul (Faust-like) to Satan. Barnes, *The Devil's Charter,* lines 3375–99.

32. Ibid., lines 1422–34. Bullbeggar was used interchangeably with "bugbear" in Samuel Harsnett, *A Declaration of Egregious Popish Impostures* (1603; STC 12880), 135–36. It refers to religious imposters, mainly Catholic, with a pun on Papal bulls. Bellarmino was called "the Pope's Bullbeggar" in 1630 (*OED*). Since bullbeggars suggest hocus-pocus, "sergeants' heads" may be apparitions like the conjurer's Brazen Head in Greene's *Friar Bacon* and the Armed Head at *Macbeth* 4.1.68ff.

33. Francis Herring, *Pietas Pontificia* (1606; STC 13244), translated by John Vicars as *The Quintessence of Cruelty* (London, 1641).

34. Adams, op, cit., 122.

35. *The Whore of Babylon* 4.2.97–98.

36. Ibid., 5.1.43–44.

37. Ibid., 5.2.45–46, 3.1.59–60. Cf. Barnes, *The Devil's Charter,* line 3218: "This train was laid of purpose for our lives."

38. *Whore* 3.1.59–60. Lancelot Andrewes said the Plotters worked by "undermining, digging deep" (op. cit., 211).

39. Ibid. 4.4.121.

40. Besides other uses of "train," already noticed, see Andrewes, op. cit., 4: 215: "All was prepared, the train, the match, the fire [dynamite], "wood" [iron bars to increase the damage] and all, and we ready to be the sacrifice [like Isaac]." Also

Dekker's 1607 pamphlet, *A Knight's Conjuring:* "[The Plotters] lay *trains* of sedition to *blow up* the commonwealth."

41. Adams, op. cit., 122.

42. The filling of the air with the Plot's debris was a continuing part of the Gunpowder myth. Within ten years of the Plot, Thomas Campion was writing in his Latin poem: "Had powder done its fated work, the whole Parliament had flown apart in air, along with the King, by a lightning bolt from Rome":

> Fataleque pulvis
> Fecerat officium, sparsusque Senatus in auras
> Fulmine Romano totus cum rege perisset.

(*De Pulveria Conjuratione,* edited by David Lindley, Leeds Texts, n.s. 10, 1987, 2. 367–69).

43. Dekker, *Whore* 4.4.55–58. The scriptural City of Confusion (Isaiah 24.10) was identified with Babel, where God confused the tongues of the impious. Since Protestant invective identified Bable with Babylon, the Pope, as the Whore of Babylon, presides over the City of Confusion.

44. Cf. Coke on the Plotters (Adams, op. cit., 116): "Howsoever they sought to shadow their impiety with the cloak of religion, yet they intended to breed *confusion* . . . . He that desires primacy upon earth shall surely find *confusion* in heaven."

45. Andrewes, op. cit., 4: 216.

46. Adams, op. cit., 167.

47. Herring, *Pietas Pontificia:*

> Rex prudens, tacita pervolvens singula mente
> Sic tandem: Indicia haec non sunt temnenda . . . .

Cf. Vicars, *Mischief's Mystery* (STC 13247):

> Yet I, a Joseph, Daniel, will procure
> T' untwine the twist of its obscurity.

By the time of Vicars's translation of Herring, Bellarmino had written an attack on James under the pseudonym *Tortus* (Turned), and Lancelot Andrewes answered him in a work called *Tortura Torti,* "The Turned Re-Turned," an untwining of the twist.

The comparison of the Plot to the Trojan Horse was one of two recurring classical references. The other one, started by the King himself, was to the Conspiracy of Catiline.

48. The power of the original writings on Plot theology can be seen in their long afterlife. The Plot as a model of diabolic enmity filled a series of short epics (*epyllia*) on the providential role of England in God's plans—Francis Herring's *Pietas Pontificia* (1606), Thomas Campion's *De Pulveria Conjuratione* (1615?), Phineas Fletcher's *Locustae* (1627). Milton considered writing an epic on the Powder Treason—and, in a sense, he did. Scholars have traced the heavy influence on *Paradise Lost* of Fletcher's own translation of *Locustae* as *The Apollyonists*. Cf. J. B. Broadbent, *Some Graver Subject* (Chatto & Windus, 1960), 96, 126, 131, 183; Stella Purce Revard, *The War in Heaven* (Cornell University Press, 1980), 87–107; David Quint, *Epic and Empire* (Princeton University Press, 1993), 270–81. Some critics of *Paradise Lost* take particular exception to the artillery forces Satan deploys against the unfallen angels. But the opportunity to show the devil inventing gunpowder had great resonance for Milton and his ideological comrades. The battle in heaven was a type of the Plot that revealed the devil's nature in British history. People in Milton's time read lines like these with Jesuits in mind, as well as devils (Book 6, lines 512–15, 586–89).

> Sulphurous and nitrous foam
> They found, they mingl'd, and (with subtle art
> Concocted and adusted) they reduc'd
> To blackest grain, and into store convey'd . . .
>
> . . . whose roar
> Embowel'd with outrageous noise the air,
> And all her entrails tore, disgorging foul
> The devilish glut . . .

Two · Witches

1. The apparent exception is Marston's *Sophonisba*, where the witch creates a love spell for Syphax. But Syphax's rivalry for Sophonisba's love is the basis of the plot that overthrows Carthage. It has been held that the witch scenes were added to *Sophonisba*, which might well be true—added for their timeliness in 1606 (Marston had been working on this learned play since 1604). See Peter Corbin and Douglas Sedge, Introduction, *Three Jacobean Witchcraft Plays* (Manchester University

Press, 1986), 6. Marston makes the general-dictator of Carthage a king so that attacks on him become regicide: "Some god's in kings, that will not let them fall" (2.3.19).

2. W. J. Adams, *The Gunpowder Treason* (London, 1851), 117.

3. Lancelot Andrewes, *Works* (Oxford: John Henry Parker, 1853), Vol. 4, p. 214.

4. Dekker, *The Whore of Babylon* 3.1.83–88.

5. Ben Jonson, *Catiline* 1.2.423–24: "We take a solemn sacrament / To strengthen our design." The "sacrament" is wine mixed with blood (1.2.484). For the connection with the Powder Treason, see B. N. De Luna, *Jonson's Romish Plot* (Clarendon Press, 1967), 173–75.

6. *"The Devil's Charter." A Critical Edition,* lines 1242–1392, 2105–8, 2651–2794. It is a sign of relaxed censorship in 1606 that Dekker could put a pederastic Pope on the stage. Overt homosexuality rarely passed the censors—the greatest other exception, involving the King's pro-French minion in Marlowe's *Edward II,* was staged at another period of laxer censorship, following on the Armada invasion. For the apologetic and cautious air with which homosexuality was treated when it did arise, see Alan Bray, *Homosexuality in Renaissance England* (Gay Men's Press, 1982), 61–62. Homosexuality was considered a particularly Italian (= papist = Jesuitical) vice in the theological disputes of the time (Bray, op. cit., 14–16, 19–21, 29). It should be remembered that the minion in *Edward II* is an instrument of the realm's dissolution. Even Bruce R. Smith, who finds Marlovian sympathy for Edward's homosexuality in the play, admits that the structural framework of the plot is satirical in its treatment of the "minion." See Smith, *Homosexual Desire in Shakespeare's England* (University of Chicago Press, 1991), 221: "His pattern of tragedy, in this play as in *Doctor Faustus,* comes from the dogmatic scheme of rewards and punishments that govern morality plays."

7. "It was the Jesuits above all who came to embody in popular mythology the identification of Popery with homosexuality" (Bray, op. cit., 20). Coke found in Plotters against the King a triple treason, "by heresy, by buggery, by sodomy" (ibid.). A playwright like Shakespeare would be especially alert to such charges, since they were leveled at the players' use of their boy actors.

> It is the custom of vagabond players that coast from town to town with a truss and a cast of broken queens and Ganymedes, as well for their night pleasance as their day's pastime. . . .

Samuel Harsnett, *A Declaration of Egregious Popish Inventions* (1603; STC 12880), 149. For boy loves as "Ganymedes," see Marston's *The Scourge of Villanie*, III, cited in Bray, op. cit., 16.

8. Harsnett, op. cit., 14. Dekker's *The Whore of Babylon* presented the Jesuits in the act of being dispatched from Rome with magical exorcism-equipment, beginning with the holy water whose use in exorcism James had mocked (*Daemonologie*, 49):

> Ere you shift air [to England],
> Sprinkle yourselves all o'er with sacred drops.
> Take periapts, pentacles, and potent charms
> To conjure down foul fiends that will be raised
> To vex you. . . . [*The Whore of Babylon* 1.1.222–26]

Compare Harsnett's attack on the exorcists' gear: "blessed beads, holy water, hallowed crosses, periapts, amulets, smocks of proof and such" (p. 138). For "smocks of proof"—vests to make one immune from diabolic influence—see Reginald Scot, *The Discoverie of Witchcraft*, Book 12, chap. 9 (Dover edition, pp. 131–32): "On Christmas day at night, a thread must be spun of flax by a little virgin girl . . . ."

9. Ibid., 127. Harsnett thought the Mass as conceived by Catholics was an exercise in magic, an attempt to "deify this bread-idol and make it a God" (p. 127). This made the Mass "a monster engine [device] of all prodigious signs, cogged miracles, and gross-heathenish concerted wonders" (ibid). Harsnett did not believe the devil had power to respond to such tricks; but that did not reduce the fact that the Jesuits gave up their souls to the devil by trying the tricks, and by seducing others with them. It is sometimes said that Harsnett, like his fellow polemicist Reginald Scot, "denied witchcraft," because both men said God would not give devils the powers claimed for them. But both men believed in the devil, and believed that those invoking him lost their souls to him despite his limited scope of intervention. In all this the Jesuits served the Pope, "His Holiness and his hellish crew" (p. 135).

10. Andrewes, op. cit., 4:215.

11. *The Jesuits' Miracles* (1606; STC 20340). The Garnet "miracle" is described below (Chapter Five).

12. This objection was stated as early as 1805 by E. H. Stevens: "The witches seem to be introduced for no other purpose than to tell us they are to meet again,

and as I cannot discover any advantage resulting from such anticipation, but, on the contrary, think it injurious, I conclude the scene is not genuine (*Variorum*, 7–8). Some directors agree, and excise the scene—including Harley Granville-Barker and Tyrone Guthrie (Rosenberg, 5, 31).

13. *Macbeth* 4.1.28–29. "The "birth-strangled babe / Ditch-deliver'd by a drab" (4.1.30–31) is unholy in every way—its whore mother kills it instead of baptizing it. See Middleton, *The Witch* 1.2.18–19.

> Take the *unbaptised* brat,
> Boil it well, preserve the fat.

Marlowe's Doctor Faustus promised to "offer lukewarm blood of new-born babes" (A 2.1.14), captured for use before they were baptized. Stealing babies from their cribs is a standard witch's crime. The dog-familiar in *The Witch of Edmonton* describes the hunt for unrepentant people's corpses (5.1.139–42):

> The old cadaver of some self-strangled wretch
> We sometimes borrow, and appear human.
> The carcase of some disease-slain strumpet
> We varnish fresh and wear as her first beauty.

14. For a collection of patristic texts (from Origen, Eustathius, and Gregory of Nyssa) on the use of Samuel's body by the witch, see Manlio Simonetti, *La maga di Endor* (Nardini Editore, 1989). It is in this theological tradition that James writes his dialogue *Daemonologie*.

15. Since the devil could "possess" the living—causing fits and dementia—but not wield their bodies at will, he turned to animals for embodying his "familiar spirits" (the witches' cats, crows, toads, etc.). Animals are more pervious, since they lack immortal souls.

16. Harsnett, op. cit., A2 verso. King James described how the devil "can put his own spirit in a dead body, which the *necromancers* commonly practise" (*Daemonologie*, 28–29). Necromancy is the first and most continuing concern of his dialogue, since it is the form of witchcraft best attested in scripture and most thoroughly explored by the fathers of the church. See, for instance:

> p. 14: "to enter in a dead body and there-out-of to give answers of the event . . . ."
> p. 41: "if they have assumed a dead body . . . to trouble the rest of a dead

body . . . . when the Devil carries it out of the grave to serve his turn for a space . . . haunting with their bodies after they are dead . . . ."

p. 50 "devils entering in the dead bodies of the faithful . . . ."

17. Ibid., 30. James knew the uses of such "jointed" body parts since they were hung on the cursed cat that almost shipwrecked his boat in 1590. See *Newes from Scotland*, reprinted in *Withcraft in England 1558–1618*, edited by Barbara Rosen (University of Massachusetts Press, 1991), 196: the witches "bound to each part of that cat the chiefest parts of a dead body."

18. Ibid., 46–47. The devil's second-hand use of human semen can be discerned, since "that sperm seems intolerably cold to the person abused."

19. I James I, c. 12 (1604), quoted in Rosen, op. cit., 57, from *Statutes of the Realm*, Vol. 4, Part 2, p. 1028.

20. John Marston, *Sophonisba* 4.1.111–21, drawing on Lucan, *Pharsalia* 6.560–68.

21. John Weever, *Ancient Funeral Monuments* (1631), 45–46. For the importance of finding the "newly dead," especially such dammed souls as died by suicide, see Scot, *Discoverie*, Book 15, chap. 8 (Dover edition, p. 232).

22. Rosen, op. cit., 58.

23. On the national scare over the discovery of a witch's doll with "Elizabeth" on its forehead, see George Lyman Kittredge, *Witchcraft in Old and New England* (Atheneum, 1972), 88. On another occasion, a doll of Elizabeth was found with a pin through its heart, and the Privy Council called on Dee to protect the Queen. Peter J. French, *John Dee: The World of an Elizabethan Magus* (Routledge & Kegan Paul, 1972), 6–7. James feared a similar threat from a wax image associated with the Earl of Bothwell's plots, and prosecuted the witches suspected of making the image: D. Harris Willson, *King James VI and I* (Jonathan Cape, 1956), 104–6.

24. *Daemonologie*, 31–32: The Devil "teacheth how to make pictures of wax or clay that, by the roasting thereof, the persons that they bear the name of may be continually melted or dried away . . . . They can bewitch and take the life of men or women by roasting of the pictures . . . ."

25. *Dictionary of National Biography*, s.v. Edward Squire.

26. *News from Scotland*, in Rosen, op. cit., 193–203.

27. Willson, op. cit., 106–13.

28. Arthur Melville Clark, *Murder Under Trust* (Scottish Academy Press, 1981), 82–83.

29. Barnes's play resembles so closely some aspects of *Macbeth* that Mark Eccles,

in his study of Barnes, supposed that "James had liked *Macbeth* and wanted another play with even more demonologie"—which Barnes provided. See Eccles, "Barnabe Barnes," p. 233, in *Thomas Lodge and Other Elizabethans*, edited by C. J. Sisson (Harvard University Press, 1933).

30. *"The Devil's Charter."* 119. William Monter points out the irony that Barnes's "Candy," Juan de Gandía, had a grandson who became a canonized Jesuit (St. Francis Borgia).

31. For Hecate in Welles's 1936 production, see Bernice W. Kliman, *Shakespeare in Performance: "Macbeth"* (Manchester University Press, 1992), 87–88; and Richard France, *The Theatre of Orson Welles* (Bucknell University Press, 1977), 58–63.

32. They are Shakespearian in the sense that they develop his own (replaced) scenes for his troupe, no matter what contributions were made by a collaborator (generally assumed to be Middleton, Shakespeare's collaborator in *Timon of Athens*). For the textual critics, see Brooke, 64–68, and Stanley Wells and Gary Taylor, *William Shakespeare: A Textual Companion* (Clarendon Press, 1987), 543–45. For performance, see Rosenberg, 490–96 (he notes a 1974 performance with a nude Hecate), and Peter Hall, "Directing *Macbeth*," in *Focus on Macbeth*, edited by John Russell Brown (Routledge & Kegan Paul, 1982), 243: "I can amass, to me, formidable reasons why Act III Scene V must be authentic . . . Without Hecate there is a static nature to the development of the witches . . . The cauldron scene should be staged as a masque, with Hecate flying." Some critics have always treated the Hecate scenes as authentic—notably J. M. Nosworthy in a series of articles and on pp. 8–53 of his *Shakespeare's Occasional Plays: Their Origin and Transmission* (Barnes & Noble, 1965) and G. Wilson Knight in *The Shakespearian Tempest* (Methuen & Co., 1953), 326–32. As Kliman (op. cit., 17) writes: "If the Hecate scenes are genuine, Shakespeare's production avoided the unified greyness of tone of modern productions. Janet Adelman's contention that 'we are entrapped in Macbeth's head as claustrophobically as he is until the scene in England' would not hold."

33. The Holinshed passages are in Geoffrey Bullough, *Narrative and Dramatic Sources of Shakespeare* (Columbia University Press, 1973), 500, 504. Shakespeare recognized the theatrical effectiveness of conjuring scenes—something proved by the scary fame of the magical incantations in *Doctor Faustus*. The other conjuring scenes in Shakespeare—La Pucelle's in *I Henry VI* and Margery Jourdain's in *II Henry VII*—are also lacking in Shakespeare's sources. Since the Folio gives only the song *cues* in 3.5 and 4.1, the song texts recovered from Middleton are not entirely reliable. The cat-costumed actor probably belonged solely to the Middleton play.

34. For the actors' numbers and deployment in the 1606 play, see below (Chapter Four).

35. Thomas Heywood and Richard Brome, *The Late Lancashire Witches*, line 447, edited by Laird H. Barber (Garland Publishing, 1949), 149.

36. Mephistopheles actually urges Faustus to flee his master, the devil (*Doctor Faustus* A 1.3.83–84). Other subordinate witches depart from their hellish assignments. Merlin, the devil's son, finally turns on his father in Rawley's *The Birth of Merlin*. The dog-familiar in *The Witch of Edmonton* whimsically lets one of his prey escape after toying with it (5.1.110–11, 192). Hecate's insubordinate son, Firestone, defies her in Middleton's *The Witch*.

37. These lines are explicated in Chapter Three.

38. *Doctor Faustus* A 1.3.83–84.

39. For more on the supernatural language of these scenes, see note 29 in Chapter Three.

40. *Doctor Faustus* B.1.3.1, 5.2.1.

41. Ibid. A 2.183–84 (p. 142). This resembles further comforting "shows" in the play (e.g., of Helen) and in others—e.g., the dog-familiar's manifestation of a fair (but fake) "Katherine" to the Younger Banks in *The Witch of Edmonton* 3.1.74ff.

42. The relation of *Macbeth* to Middleton's *The Witch* is not a question that can be settled in our present state of knowledge. There is good reason to suspect the normal account of the matter, which runs like this: sometime before *Macbeth* took its present shape, Middleton wrote *The Witch*, which was a failure on the stage—so the King's Men salvaged the play's two songs for use when Hecate appears in *Macbeth* 3.5 and 4.1. But the assumption that *The Witch* failed in performance is a shaky one, according to Anne Lancashire. Middleton gave the (now lost) manuscript of the play to a friend, with a claim that he had a hard time retrieving it himself and that it was an "ignorant-ill-fated labor of mine." (We have only copies of this lost manuscript written in the 1620s—the play became known to the public in 1778.) Lancashire argues that *The Witch* was not a failure with audiences but with the "ignorant" censors, since the plot of the drama so obviously refers to the scandalous 1613 divorce of Robert Devereux by Frances Howard—a divorce King James promoted by endorsing the wife's claim that her husband had been made impotent by his dealings with witches. If a license was denied the play, it would have been dangerous as well as difficult to circulate it. If *The Witch* was written circa 1613, the play's songs could have been incorporated in *Macbeth* after its license was refused. But, as Brooke points out, Middleton (or another) could also have written

the songs before 1613, for a relicensed *Macbeth* with new casting provisions. How-ever the elements of the Folio text came together, it is as close as we can get to Shakespeare's play in Shakespeare's time. See Anne Lancashire, *"The Witch: Stage Flop or Political Mistake?"* in *"Accompaninge the Players." Essays Celebrating Thomas Middleton, 1580–1980,* edited by Kenneth Friedenreich (AMS Press, 1983), 161–81. The date of the *Macbeth* revision is discussed in Appendix One.

Three · Male Witch

1. David Bradley, *From Text to Performance in the Elizabethan Theatre* (Cambridge University Press, 1992), 27–28. The whole first chapter, "The Logic of Entrances," is relevant. It is true that a character can step out from the discovery space under the stage gallery; but that is unsettling for people who meet out of doors (like the witches) since the discovery space is mainly used to suggest interiors.

2. *Daemonologie*, 27.

3. Richard Burton, *The Anatomy of Melancholy* (1628), edited by Floyd Dell and Paul Jordan (Tudor Publishing Co., 1927), 209 (ii 1.2.5). See in the same passage: "A thick air thickeneth the blood and humors . . . Polydore calls it a *filthy* sky."

4. The normal way of performing the line, "Hŏvĕř thrŏugh thĕ fóg . . ." provides a weak ending to the scene. The meter is meant to stress the physical *lean* of the witches on the sustaining ("filthy") air. Ben Jonson used a similarly metered line to end the witches' song in *The Masque of Queens,* lines 276–78, in *The Complete Masques,* edited by Stephen Orgel (Yale University Press, 1969), 265:

> Seas roar, woods roll,
> Clouds crack, all be black
> Bŭt thĕ líght oŭr chásms do make.

Compare: "Hŏvĕř thróugh thĕ fóg . . ."

5. Lancelot Andrewes, *Works* (Oxford University Press, 1853), Vol. 7, 207–8.

6. Erichtho, in Marston's play, prefers nights when "dark winds / Or thick black clouds drive back the blinded stars" (4.1.104–5). For night as itself a potion that brews evil into things for further "cooking," see the classical references collected by C.D.N. Costa, *Seneca, "Medea"* (Clarendon Press, 1989), 134.

7. *II Henry VI* 1.4.15–16, 20.

8. *Doctor Faustus* A1.3.1–5. Vergil's *nimbrosus Orion* ("drizzly Orion") at *Aeneid* 1.535 indicates a special time of *year* as well as *day*—the period of autumn storms.

Notes

See note at W. W. Greg, *Marlowe's Doctor Faustus: 1604–1616: Parallel Texts* (Clarendon Press, 1950), 360.

9. *Macbeth* 1.5.50–54, and *Daemonologie*, 27.

10. Glenn Byam Shaw carefully observed these indications of time in his 1955 production of the first four scenes. *"Macbeth" Onstage: An Annotated Facsimile of Glenn Byam Shaw's 1955 Promptbook*, edited by Michael Mullin (University of Missouri Press, 1976), 23–24.

11. Pope's emendation of F *sides* to *strides* is generally accepted, though *sights* is a near-homophone. Tarquin has "sights toward his design." He moves with his rape "in view." See *A Lover's Complaint*, 282, where a man's "sights till then were level'd on my face" (plural "sights" of a singular agent). The punctuation of *Macbeth*'s line 55 should contrast Murder's generalized movement with the specific way Tarquin stalks Lucrece.

12. For abuse as the devil's abuse of nature, see *Daemonologie*, 39 ("abusing of the soul"), 40 ("abusing the more of mankind"), 46 ("abusing of men or women"), and the three uses on p. 47.

13. Brabantio brings his formal charge of witchcraft by using the term "abuse" three times—1.2.78, and also 1.2.73–74 ("with foul charms / Abus'd her delicate youth"), and 1.3.60 (Desdemona was "abus'd, stol'n from me"). He also uses "spells" (1.3.6), "witchcraft" (1.3.64), "conjuring" (1.3.105), and "practises of cunning hell" (1.3.103) to describe Othello's activities.

14. The devilish Richard III is called "self-misus'd" (4.4.374). Macbeth's eerie ("strange") mistreatment of himself is suggested by the complex of words Shakespeare sometimes creates with *self*-compounds. Lady Macbeth dies "by self-and-violent hands" (5.9.76). Ajax is "strange-or-self-affected" (i.e., not just strange but strange-affected by being self-affected) at *Troilus* 2.3.39. Goneril is "changed-and-self-cover'd" (made something other than herself by the disguising of herself) at *Lear* 4.2.62.

15. Milton, in his Latin poem on the Powder Treason, has the Devil visit Murder's lair, where "the ground, aware of the blood it rots in, lets out a moan": *Exululat tellus et sanguine conscia stagnat* (150).

16. The witch Stadlin feeds her bat-familiar from the devil's mark on her lip in Middleton's *The Witch* 3.3.7–8:

> There was a bat hung at my lips three times,
> As we came through the woods, and drank her fill.

The bat is female in Middleton, male in Macbeth's speech.

17. The West passage is in C. L'Estrange Ewen, *Witch Hunting and Witch Trials* (Kegan Paul, 1929), 22.

18. See Barbara Rosen's introduction to *Witchcraft in England, 1558–1618* (University of Massachusetts Press, 1969), 18–19.

19. King James endorsed the test of witches by "fleeting" in water (to see if they will float) since the witches had renounced their baptism (*Daemonologie, 56*):

> God hath appointed, for a supernatural sign of the monstrous impiety of the witches, that the water shall refuse to receive them in her bosom that have shaken off them the sacred water of baptism and wilfully refuse the benefit thereof.

Reginald Scot says that belief in the power of baptismal water was so great that witches tried to suck it off corpses (*The Discovery of Witchcraft*, Book 3, chap. 2, Dover edition, 24). But witches' normal traffic is with the *unbaptized* dead, as we saw in Chapter Two above. The opposition to that Bond is an omnipresent assumption of the witch literature.

20. Samuel Harsnett, *A Declaration of Egregious Popish Impostures* (1605; STC 12880), 83.

21. Robert Burton, op. cit., 174–75 (i.2.2): "This humor of melancholy is called the Devil's Bath . . . [since] melancholy persons are most subject to diabolical temptations and illusions, and most apt to entertain them, and the Devil best able to work upon them." King James, somewhat melancholy himself, denied any connection between that humor and the devil (*Daemonologie, 21*).

22. For the astrological term, see *Lear* 1.2.123 ("spherical predominance"), *All's Well* 1.1.193–94 (Mars as predominant or retrograde), and *Winter's Tale* 1.2.202 (on planets that "strike," or afflict, when predominant).

23. Just as the witches met to say they will gather again in the play's first scene, then hurried off to their business, so Hecate hovers by (in the gallery) to tell the witches they must meet again with Macbeth in the morning.

24. Some have asked how Macbeth knows where to find the witches. That is bewildering only if we presume that the witches must be searched out on the *heath*. In Holinshed, the sisters live "in a house in Forres"—they are, literally, sisters who share a home, which would be feared and pointed out like any "haunted house." The homes of wizards and cunning folk are dangerous places. One has to know about them, if only to avoid them. That the witches are in a house emerges from

their call to its magic locks to open themselves when Macbeth's presence has been sensed: "Open, locks!—whoever knocks" (4.1.47). There is no "hell porter" here to obstruct entry. The meeting at the witches' house seems to conflict with Hecate's instruction to meet at "the pit of Acheron" (3.5.15). But that expression is figurative in any case. They are not literally descending into hell. Acheron is *created* by the conjuring, which the witches can do in their home, just as Pope Alexander does it in his study.

25. Ovid, *Metamorphoses* 7.192. Arthur Golding expanded the Latin into "O trusty time of Night / Most faithful unto privities" (7.258-59). Here as elsewhere, Shakespeare seems to be working from the Latin, not the English. For *arcana* as secret things in Shakespeare, see Prospero "rapt in secret studies" (*Tempest* 1.2.77) and the soothsayer versed "in nature's infinite book of secrecy" (*Antony* 1.2.10).

26. The speeches are at Ovid, *Metamorphoses* 7.192-209 and Seneca, *Medea*, 750-69. Prospero's speech is at *Tempest* 5.1.33-50. It has been generally recognized that Shakespeare works at least as much from Ovid's Latin as from Golding's translation in the *Tempest* speech. (See Appendix D to Frank Kermode's Arden edition of *The Tempest*, 147-50.) The same is true for Medea's famous speech in Seneca, used in *Macbeth*. Middleton simply incorporated the original conjuring Latin of Ovid into Hecate's conjuring speech in *The Witch of Edmonton* 5.2.18-25.

27. For the relation of Medea's speech to other depictions of witches in classical antiquity, see C. D. N. Costa, op. cit., 139-44.

28. Ben Jonson, *The Masque of Queens*, lines 213-20, in Orgel, op cit., 130. There are many such lists of *adynata* in witch plays of the time. Robert Greene's friar, the legendary inventer of gunpowder (with the devil's collaboration), boasts at *Friar Bacon* 2.46-51:

> Resolve you, doctors, Bacon can by books
> Make storming Boreas thunder from his cave
> And dim fair Luna to a dark eclipse.
> The great arch-ruler, potentate of hell
> Trembles when Bacon bids him or his fiends
> Bow to the force of his pentageron [pentagram].

29. For the items in the witch repertoire of *adynata*, compare Macbeth's list with Medea's boasts in Ovid, *Metamorphoses* 7 and Senaca's *Medea:*

Untie the winds: Ovid 202 *ventos abigoque vocoque.*

Yesty waves confound: Seneca 765 *Sonuere fluctus, tumuit insanum mare*

bladed corn be lodg'd: Seneca 761 *coacta messem vidit hibernam Ceres*

trees blown down: Ovid 205 *silvas moveo*

castles topple, pyramids and palaces slope to their foundations: Ovid 205 *jubeoque tremescere montes,* Seneca 769 *Hyadesque nostris cantibus motae labant.* "Slope" seems to echo *labant.*

nature's germen tumble all together: Seneca 757–58 *Mundus lege confusa aetheris / Et solem et astra vidit*

till destruction sicken: Ovid 209 *pallet nostris Aurora venenis*

30. The ingredients of Medea's "foaming cauldron" are as foul and exotic as those of *Macbeth*'s witches—guts of werewolf, wing of owl, head of raven, etc. (*Metamorphoses* 7.262–78). Seneca's witch, true to form, uses head of owl and plants clipped at midnight (*Medea* 729–34). Compare the *alta nocte succisus frutex* (729) with "slips of yew / Sliver'd in the moon's eclipse" (*Macbeth* 4.1.28–29).

31. *Antony* 5.2.348, *Caesar* 2.1.206. See also *Hamlet* 3.2.347, *Love's Labour's* 4.3.2.

32. E. K. Chambers gives four different written reports of diabolic activity feared or actually occurring during the conjuring scene of *Doctor Faustus* (E. K. Chambers, *Elizabethan Stage* (Oxford University Press, 1967), Vol. 3, 423–24).

33. The *torturing* of God's name is the supreme example of the way magicians force nature out of its course, *abuse* it. Greene's Friar Bacon says he will *"strain out nigromancy to the deep"* (2.54). This is a *"wresting* of the holy name of God" (13.92). In Jonson's *The Alchemist,* a magician is called a "persecutor of nature" (1.3.100), some one who can "fink [pen] nature up in her own center" (2.1.28). Since the Hebrew printing of God's name already omitted the word's vowels, as an apotropaic euphemism, this "code word" stood partway toward detaching names from heavenly protection. The four consonants made up the tetragrammaton (JHVH) that could be "racked" on the pentagram inscribed in or around magic circles. This complex of signs was made to represent the universe when brought into mystical alignment with the stars through astrology. The intricate formulae resulting are exemplified by the drawings in Reginald Scot's *Discoverie,* Book 15, chaps. 6 and 7 (Dover edition, 228–32). The 1619 frontispiece to the B Quarto of *Doctor Faustus* shows how the ground was marked off as an inverse of *sacred* precincts (Frontispiece).

34. *The Devil's Charter*, lines 1895–96.

35. Ibid., lines 1851–55, 1902–3.

36. Jonson, *The Masque of Queens*, lines 327–31 (Orgel, 134).

37. Rosenberg, *Masks*, 516.

38. Since Macbeth first sees the ghost seated, many assume that the chair with Banquo on it rises from the trap. But the Folio clearly says *"Enter the Ghost of Banquo, and sits in Macbeth's place. . . . Exit Ghost . . . Enter Ghost . . . Exit Ghost."* Some think *enter* can be a general term to cover "appears" in all its senses. But the directions clearly indicate two separate acts—the ghost enters *and* (then) sits. Simon Forman also reported that, "the ghost of Banquo came and sat down" (Brooke, p. 236). See also Peter Hall, interviewed in *Focus on Macbeth*, edited by John Russell Brown (Routledge & Kegan Paul, 1982), 245: "Some directors try to hide the moment when Banquo's ghost comes on stage, but I think his entry is very well marked in the rhythm of the text. I am sure he just walks on."

39. The sanctity of marriage, for instance, puts it outside diabolic tampering, a point made by Mephistopheles (*Doctor Faustus* A 2.1.146–55) and by Hecate in Middleton's *The Witch* (1.2.172–77):

> We cannot disjoin wedlock.
> 'Tis of heaven's fastening. Well may we raise jars,
> Jealousies, strifes, and heart-burning disagreements
> Like a thick scurf o'er life, as did our master
> Upon that patient miracle [Job], but the work itself
> Our power cannot disjoint.

40. The most famous irony is in the feigned yet real sorrow Macbeth expresses to others after Duncan's corpse is discovered (2.3.91–92):

> Had I but died an hour before this chance,
> I had liv'd a blessed time.

See Chapter Five on truth *beneath* this play's lies.

41. Peter Stallybrass, "*Macbeth* and Witchcraft," in *Focus on "Macbeth,"* 200.

42. Rosenberg, 512.

43. Dennis Bartholomeusz, *Macbeth and the Players* (Cambridge University Press, 1969), 154–70.

44. The other conjurers are the Duchess of Gloucester, Margery Jourdain, and

Joan La Pucelle. Macbeth and the witches in *Macbeth* complete the count of Shakespeare's occult criminals.

45. Campeius is a scholar, like Faustus ("A soul within him fram'd of a thousand wheels," 2.1.189), who bargains with the agents of the whore to satisfy his ambition (2.2.154).

> Thus to meet heaven, who would not wade through hell?

46. Harsnett, op. cit., 14, on the "devil-conjuring priests."

Four · Lady Macbeth

1. Line counts for the various roles are taken from the tables in T. J. King, *Casting Shakespeare's Plays: London Actors and Their Roles* (Cambridge University Press, 1992). They come to 263 lines for Lady Macbeth, by contrast with 693 for Cleopatra and 557 for Portia.

2. Boy actors of the requisite diction, memory, and ability to sing and dance were hard to come by in the public theater, where their very presence was under continual assault by moralists (see Chapter 2, note 7). Good boy performers had a short time to learn and perfect their skills before losing the female parts when their voices changed. Shakespeare's great termagant roles of the early 1590s, and his roles for a matched comic pair (a tall boy and a short boy) in the middle nineties, indicate how Shakespeare tailored parts for the troupe's apprentices—as he did for its clowns, and for Burbage himself.

3. See note 28 below.

4. E. K. Chambers, *The Elizabethan Stage* (Oxford University Press, 1967), Vol. 2, p. 213.

5. One of the Merchant Taylors' men was paid thirteen shillings "for things for the boys that made the speech, viz. for garters, stockings, shoes, ribbons, and gloves." The Merchant Taylors Company's account books cited in Gerald Eades Bentley, *The Profession of Player in Shakespeare's Time, 1590–1642* (Princeton University Press, 1984), 126.

6. Compare the coaching of Moth, the "pretty knavish page," in *Love's Labour's* 5.2.98–99:

> Action and account did they teach him there.
> "Thus must thou speak," and "Thus thy body bear."

7. Chambers, op. cit., 4: 72.

8. That Rice was still performing as a boy in 1610 means that he was probably no older than thirteen in 1607. The prime of a boy's acting years is illustrated in the case of John Honeyman, who played a woman in *The Roman Actor* when he was thirteen, and in *The Deserving Favorite* and *The Picture* when he was sixteen, but changed to an adult male part in *The Soddered Citizen* when he turned seventeen (King, op. cit., 77, 117, 119, 121, 122).

9. See Appendix One.

10. Antony twice calls Cleopatra a "witch" (at 4.2.37 and 4.12.47). Her soothsayer is called a male witch (1.2.40). Antony also calls her a "gypsy," another word for witch (4.12.28), and cries, "These strong Egyptian fetters I must break" (1.2.116). For the connection of gypsy magic with Egypt, see Othello on his charmed handkerchief (3.4.56) and the reference to Egyptian magic at *Pericles* 3.2.84–86. Cleopatra is an "enchanting" figure (1.2.128) who makes Antony "the noble ruin of her magic" (3.10.18). Pompey describes her power over him (2.1.20–23):

> All the *charms* of love,
> Salt Cleopatra, soften they wan'd lip!
> Let *witchcraft* join with beauty, lust with both.
> *Tie up* the libertine. . . .

Binding and *tying* were the work of magic. Spells *chain* the enthralled—as Brabantio says Desdemona was charmed by Othello's spells ("if she in *chains* of *magic* were not *bound*," *Othello* 1.2.65). Antony bids Cleopatra to "chain mine arm'd neck," to leap into his breast and ride on its panting sighs (4.8.14–16)—like a witch riding the air. See also Chapman, *Homer's "Odysses"* 10.500: "Dissolve the charms that their forc'd forms enchain" (said of Circe's bewitchment of Odysseus' men).

11. *Macbeth* 1.5.43–46. The thickening of blood, to stop its flow, was attributed to the black "humor" that caused both melancholy and diabolic incursions into the human system (see Chapter 3, note 3). Cf. *King John* 3.2.42–43: "that surly spirit, Melancholy / Had bak'd thy blood and made it heavy, thick . . . ." The "baked blood" keeps out mirth in the *King John* passage, as it keeps out compunction in Lady Macbeth's dark prayer.

12. Mark Rose claimed that Lady Macbeth "practises witchcraft" (*Shakespearean Design*, Harvard University Press, 1972, 88). W. Moelwyn Merchant described "Lady Macbeth's willed submission to demonic power, her unequivocal resolve to lay her being open to the invasion of witchcraft" (*Aspects of Macbeth*, edited by Kenneth Muir and Philip Edwards (Cambridge University Press, 1977), 51).

13. The witches hovered near Lady Macbeth in a 1964 Austrian production of the play (Rosenberg, 201). For the same actress doubling the Lady and Hecate, see ibid., 492.

14. For ministers as angels, see Isabella's prayer at *Measure for Measure* 5.1.115: "Then, O you blessed ministers above . . . ." See also Laertes's "A minist'ring angel shall my sister be" (*Hamlet* 5.1.248). For devils as ministers, see "minister of hell" at *I Henry VI* 5.4.93 and *Richard III* 1.2.46, and Sycorax's "potent ministers" at *Tempest* 1.2.275. Prospero's intermediate spirits are "ministers of fate" (*Tempest* 3.3.61, 65, 87).

15. "Take" can mean "blast" or "wither," a witch-usage as at *Merry Wives* 4.4.31 (the phantom "blasts the trees and *takes* the cattle") or *Hamlet* 1.1.163–64, on the blessed Christmas time:

> then no planets strike
> No fairy *takes*, nor witch hath power to charm.

Or the verb can mean *take in exchange for*—her milk becomes the watery "gall" that ran when witches' marks were cut into. A witch named Alice Samuels had her mark cut open in 1593, and it ran "yellow with milk and water," then clear (non-white) "milk," then blood. See C. L'Estrange Ewen, *Witchcraft and Demonianism* (Heath Cranton Ltd., 1933), 173.

16. See *Newes from Scotland* (1591): "the Devil doth generally mark them with a privy mark, by reason the witches have confessed themselves that the Devil doth lick them with his tongue in some privy part of their body before he doth receive them to be his servants" (Barbara Rosen, *Witchcraft in England: 1558–1618* (University of Massachusetts Press, 1991), 194).

17. Joan fed several devils at once, since witches often had multiple mole-teats. Margaret Wyard confessed in 1645 that "she had seven imps like flies, dors [bees], spiders, mice, and she had but five teats, and when they came to suck, they fight like pigs with a sow." C. L'Estrange Ewen, *Witch Hunting and Witch Trials* (Kegan Paul, 1929), 306. Since devils were bodiless spirits, they could appear to men only if they created phantasms of "thick air," spoke through dead human bodies, or used live animals' bodies. They could use human semen in incubus-intercourse, but they had to take it from animals' bodies to have real physical coupling. When Lady Macbeth invokes the murthering ministers' "sightless [invisible] substances" at 1.5.49, she is referring to demons who have not taken familiars' animal bodies.

18. They also use their familiars to suck the life from others—the fair Rosa-

mund was killed by toads, acting under orders from their witch. See George Lyman Kittredge, *Witchcraft in Old and New England* (Atheneum, 1972), 182–83. The conjurer-pope in Barnes's play uses serpents at the breast to kill his pederastic victims (lines 2770–89). The evil Queen Elinor in Peele's *Edward I* (lines 2094–96) kills a critic of her acts the same way.

19. Compare the "fatal raven" of *Titus* 2.3.97.

20. King John in the play is given two portents (two *adynata*) to assure him, just as Macbeth was. John will not fall until stones fight men and birds defeat armies. Then, to a deafening clamor of birds sent ahead of the French army, the earth is darkened and the English army breaks and runs, done in by "a flight of ugly ravens." Cf. *The Raigne of King Edward III*, edited by Fred Lapides (Garland Publishing, 1980). The ravens "made at noon a night unnatural / Upon the quaking and dismayed world"—like "night's predominance . . . When living light should kiss [the earth] at *Macbeth* 3.4.8–9. The ravens fly in "corner'd squares," like the "brave squares of battle" at *Antony* 3.11.4 or "our squares of battle" at *Henry V* 4.2.28. For the possibility of Shakespearean authorship, see Kenneth Muir, *Shakespeare as Collaborator* (Barnes & Noble, 1960), 10–55, and Stanley Wells and Gary Taylor, *William Shakespeare: A Textual Companion* (Clarendon Press, 1987), 136–37.

21. Harpy, from Greek *harpazein*, to snatch, corresponded with the Jacobean word "gripe" for carrion birds. (This word is used for Seneca's *vultur* in the Elizabethan translations.) "Harpyr" at *I Tamburlaine* 2.7.56 is emended to "harpy" by Marlowe's editors.

22. Ben Jonson, *Works*, edited by C. H. Herford (Oxford University Press, 1941), Vol. 7, 23.

23. Ben Jonson, *The Complete Masques*, edited by Stephen Orgel (Yale University Press, 1969), 127 (lines 142–45), with Jonson's own note at 532–33.

24. *"Macbeth" Onstage: An Annotated Facsimile of Glen Byam Shaw's 1955 Promptbook*, edited by Michael Mullin (University of Missouri Press, 1976), 113, 131.

25. Richard David, "The Tragic Curve," *Shakespeare Survey* 9 (1956): 129.

26. Ibid.

27. None of the plays Shakespeare's troupe acted in the 1606–07 Christmas-to-Lent season needs more than three boys. In *Macbeth*, if Hecate appeared with three *boys* as the witches, that would make four women on the stage at once—an additional reason for concluding that the witches were played by men. The first witch would most likely be played by the expert in grotesque roles, Robert Armin, who would also double the Porter. In only two scenes are two boy actors on the

stage at the same time—Lady Macduff with her son, and the sleepwalking Lady Macbeth with her woman attendant. In widely separated scenes, the same boy could play Macduff's son and the woman attendant. The shortage of boy actors in the public theater could be filled in private performances, where choristers were recruited for the large number of female roles in (for instance) *A Midsummer Night's Dream.* But in the festive calendar of the 1606–07 "twelve days of Christmas," choirs and boy performers would have their own events to prepare for, making them unavailable to the public players.

28. For Poel's Rule, see David Bradley, *From Test to Performance in the Elizabethan Theatre* (Cambridge University Press, 1992), 18. This forbids the most famous thematic doubling of the modern stage—Peter Brook's use of the same pair of actors to play Theseus with Hippolyta and Oberon with Titania. It does not interfere with the most famous *supposed* doubling, that of Cordelia and the Fool in *King Lear.* The long absence of each character from the action is hard to explain *except* by doubling. According to this theory, Lear's calling Cordelia his fool at 5.3.305 is an author's slip that confuses the actor's two roles. See Richard Abrams, "The Double Casting of Cordelia and Lear's Fool," *Texas Studies in Literature and Language* 27 (1985): 354–77. Armin, the regular fool, could play the grotesque part of "mad" Edgar.

29. See Bernice W. Kliman, *Shakespeare in Performance: "Macbeth"* (Manchester University Press, 1992), 100.

30. The shortage of boy actors helps explain another overworked mystery of the play—why Lady Macbeth's child or children do not appear. (Macduff's anguished "He has no children" is said to Malcolm, at that moment giving him cold comfort.) When Lady Macbeth says she has given suck, there is no reason to doubt her. Her husband says "Bring forth men-children only" (1.7.72)—something he could not say if she had already brought forth a girl child, but could if she had borne at least one son. Macbeth's frenzy at the thought of Banquo's heirs inheriting would be baseless if Macbeth had no heir to be supplanted. The progeny are mentioned but not dwelt on as a matter of theatrical economy. The same consideration explains why one child stands for Macduff's "children" in the murder scene (4.2).

31. *Chronicle of London,* quoted in C. L'Estrange Ewen, *Witch Hunting,* 40.

32. See, for instance, *Newes from Scotland* (in Rosen, op. cit., 193): "They, suspecting that she had been marked by the Devil, as commonly witches are, made diligent search about her and found the Enemy's mark to be in her forecrag (or forepart) of her throat. Which being found, she confessed . . . ."

Notes

33. C. L'Estrange Ewen, *Witchcraft*, 177. Even birthmarks could be a sign of a curse on certain people's offspring—like Richard III's portentous teeth formed in the womb (*Richard III* 4.4.49) or the "Vicious mole in nature" of the *Hamlet* Quarto (1.4.24) that predisposes its bearer to evil. Some held that people were marked at their birth hour by their stars' influence, and the astrologer Simon Forman noted his clients' markings when casting their horoscope—for instance: "She hath a wart or mole in the pit of her throat, or near it . . . She hath a wart under her right cheek" (Simon documents in A. L. Rowse, *Sex and Society in Shakespeare's Age* (Charles Scribner's Sons, 1974), 100, 207). The magic avoidance of such blots is the gift of Oberon to the offspring of Theseus and Hippolyta (*Midsummer Night's Dream* 5.1.395–400):

> And the blots of Nature's hand
> Shall not in their issue stand.
> Never mole, harelip, nor scar,
> Nor marks prodigious, such as are
> Despised in nativity,
> Shall upon their children be.

Five · Jesuits

1. That copy, marked by Edward Coke for his use in the prosecution of the Plotters, is now in the Bodleian Library at Oxford. The other extant copy, once in the possession of Robert Persons in Spain, now rests in the Jesuit archives at Rome. Since the copy Coke used was copied out by someone other than Garnet, the authorship of the *Treatise* was not known; but Garnet made additions and changes in his own hand, so it was clear that some connection existed between Tresham and Garnet (though Tresham at first denied having seen Garnet in the preceding sixteen years). The only publication of the manuscript was made by David Jardine, in 1851. Jardine, too, did not realize that Garnet was the author; so this crucial work has rarely been cited in discussions of the Gunpowder Plot, the Jesuits, and equivocation. See A. E. Malloch, "Father Henry Garnet's Treatise of Equivocation," *Recusant History* 15 (1981): 387–95.

2. Robert Abbott, quoted in Philip Caraman, *Henry Garnet, 1555–1606* (Farrar, Straus, 1964), 351.

3. The equivocation of these underground faiths has been studied by Perez

Zagorin in *Ways of Lying: Dissimulation, Persecution, and Conformity in Early Modern Europe* (Harvard University Press, 1990), 38–152.

4. Leonard W. Levy, *Origins of the Fifth Amendment* (Oxford University Press, 1968), 93–94.

5. Ibid., 102–5. Four members of the court endorsed Tresham's principle, but not for a Star Court proceeding (which his trial was). Tresham served twenty months in prison. Released, he went on to act in the Powder Plot, and died for that.

6. Sissela Bok, *Lying* (Pantheon, 1978), 33–46. Luther, Calvin, Pascal—all Augustinians—retained this absolutism about lies.

7. S. J. Tambiah, "The Magical Power of Words," *man* n.s. 3 (1968): 183. Jane Donawerth points out that there was another view of language available in Shakespeare's day—the one reflected in Juliet's skeptical "What's in a name?" But believers in witchcraft took the older "magical" conception of language, reflected in *both* sides of the controversy over the Gunpowder Plot. For this "magical" view of words' innate power, see Donawerth herself, *Shakespeare and the Sixteenth-Century Study of Language* (University of Illinois Press, 1984), 25–26.

8. *Treatise* (Jardine edition), 74–75. *Apud homines cor ex verbis, apud Deum vero verba pensantur ex corde.* See Albert R. Jonsen and Stephen Toulmin, *The Abuse of Casuistry: A History of Moral Reasoning* (University of California Press, 1988), 200, 211, 213, for propositions formulated *ad deum.*

9. Asked if a priest is in the house, one can answer in Latin *"non est"* (he is not) but intend "he is not eating" (*est* from *edere*, not from *esse*), Garnet, *Treatise*, 29. Or, asked to say "I swear" (*juro*) one can say "I'm hot" (*uro*) and listeners will not know the difference (ibid., 52).

10. Robert Persons wrote, in "The Resolution of Cases [of Conscience] of the English Nation" (1580s), that "if these priests are interrogated by anyone about their names, they may reply by using the names that they took when they entered religion and say that they are their own names." Text contained in P. J. Holmes, *Elizabethan Casuistry* (Catholic Record Society, 1981), 64.

11. Edward Spenser, *The Faerie Queene* 5.9.6, 11, 13, 17. For Spenser and the Jesuits, see Josephine Waters Bennett, *The Evolution of "The Fairie Queene"* (University of Chicago Press, 1942), 188–89.

12. The devil was famous for his ability to turn black to white and vice versa. The actor playing the dog-familiar in *The Witch of Edmonton* had two dog costumes, one black, one white, for his different scenes. The devil, he explains, "has the back

of a sheep, but the belly of an otter" (5.1.42–43). La Pucelle says her spirits changed her from a black peasant to a white enchantress (*I Henry VI* 1.2.84–86):

> And whereas I was black and swart before,
> With those clear rays which she infus'd on me,
> That beauty am I blest with which you see.

When Hecate's spirits conjure at *Macbeth* 4.1.44–45, this muster is called:

> Black spirits and white, red spirits and gray,
> Mingle, mingle, mingle . . .

Dekker would recognize the diabolic kinship with Jesuits ("He's brown, he's grey, he's black, he's white"). Macbeth himself refers to this skill of the devil when he says to the pale servant "The devil damn thee black, thou cream-fac'd loon" (5.3.11).

13. Double speaking is like double dealing. For "double tongues," see *Much Ado* 5.1.169, *Love's Labour's* 5.2.245. For "double dealers," *Romeo* 2.4.168 *Twelfth Night* 5.1.29, 35, *Much Ado* 5.4.114. See Sir Thomas Wyatt, "Against deceit and doubleness / What 'vaileth truth?" (Wyatt, *Collected Poems*, edited by Kenneth Muir and Patricia Thomson (Liverpool University Press, 1969), 2).

14. See, for instance, Frank L. Huntley, "*Macbeth* and the Background of Jesuitical Equivocation," *Proceedings of the Modern Language Association* 79 (1964): 390–400; Steven Mullaney, "Lying Like Truth: Riddle, Representation and Treason in Renaissance England," *ELH* 47 (1980): 320–47; William O. Scott, "Macbeth's— and Our—Self-Equivocations," *Shakespeare Quarterly* 37 (1986), 160–74; Camille Wells Slights, *The Casuistical Tradition in Shakespeare, Donne, Herbert, and Milton* (Princeton University Press, 1981), 106–32; G. I. Duthie, "Antithesis in *Macbeth*," *Shakespeare Survey* 19 (1966): 25–33; Lawrence Danson, *Tragic Alphabet* (Yale University Press, 1974), 122–41.

15. The word "equivocate" is used six times in *Macbeth* as opposed to once (*Hamlet* 5.1.138) in all the other plays. ("Equivocal" is used twice, at *All's Well* 5.3.250 and *Othello* 1.3.217.)

16. The article usually cited to establish that the Porter comes from the Mystery cycle is Glynne Wickham, "Hell-Castle and Its Door-Keeper," *Shakespeare Survey* 19 (1966): 68–74.

17. See *Friar Bacon and Friar Bungay* 16.44 (Revels Edition). Dekker, *A Knight's Conjuring*, quoted on page 143 of Marianne Gateson Riely's edition of *The Whore of Babylon* (Garland Publishing, 1980). Dekker, *The Double P* (1606; STC 6498).

18. For Armin as the Porter, see David Wiles, *Shakespeare's Clowns* (Cambridge University Press, 1987), 151, 161.

19. In this play full of threes, many of Shakespeare's trinities were given by his source—three witches, three self-accusations by Malcolm, etc. But Shakespeare invented the Porter scene, and gave it a ritual force by having the man minister to *three* of hell's "initiates," and invoke at each greeting a different devil.

20. It should be remembered that the Porter's gate of hell *is* the same portal through which Lady Macbeth welcomed Duncan's "fatal enterance" (1.5.39). He passes "under my battlements" after being deceived by the castle's pleasant aspect. In that sense, Duncan—murdered just before the Porter is wakened—walked "the primrose way" to this infernal place, already marked out by the raven's cry.

21. For the importance of the Bishop's Bible in Shakespeare, see Richmond Noble, *Shakespeare's Biblical Knowledge* (Octagon Books reprint, 1970), 69–76.

22. Richard Simpson, *Edmund Campion* (Williams and Norgate, 1867), 322.

23. Samuel Harsnett, *A Declaration of Egregious Popish Impostures* (1603; STC 12880), 82–83.

24. Caraman, op. cit., 430–32.

25. Ibid., 435.

26. Caraman (ibid., 444) quotes a report that the straw was taken to the Spanish Ambassador for safe keeping after the hunt for it began.

27. H. L. Rogers, "An English Tailor and Father Garnet's Straw," *Review of English Studies*, 1965, 44–49. The relevant part of the poem *The Jesuits' Miracles* runs:

> For when he [Garnet] died—oh! thing most strange to tell!—
> To a tailor's wife a *skipping silkman* bears
> A straw whereof [whereon] blood from a traitor fell.
> She thereon weeps ruthful devotion's tears.
> To sight thereof she then her husband brings,
> And over it a mournful dirge he sings.
>
> This holy relic whilst (they say) she kept,
> Some craftier knave than her poor plain *goseman*
> To see that straw, devoutly *stealing*, crept
> And well to search each part thereof began.

28. See the illustration in Caraman, 445.

29. Leeds Barroll, *Politics, Plague, and Shakespeare's Theater* (Cornell University Press, 1991), 143–44, 147–48.

30. This would be another argument against H. N. Paul's dating of the play to August of 1606. See Appendix One.

Six · Malcolm

1. For Walsingham's spy system, which Conyer Read says was not as extensive as legend makes it, but was, nevertheless, efficient, see Read, *Mr. Secretary Walsingham* (Clarendon Press, 1925), Vol. 2, pp. 34–43. David Lloyd claims that Walsingham "Outdid the Jesuits in their own bow and overreached them in their own equivocation" (Read, p. 341). For Cecil's assurance to James that he would extirpate Jesuits, see Mark Nicholls, *Investigating Gunpowder Plot* (Manchester University Press, 1991), 131–32.

2. King James I and VI, *Basilikon Doron* (1616), in Charles Howard McIlwain, *The Political Works of James I* (Harvard University Press, 1918), 33.

3. See, for instance, Josephine Watson Bennett, *Measure for Measure as Royal Entertainment* (Cornell University Press, 1966); and Jonathan Goldberg, *James I and the Politics of Literature* (Stanford University Press, 1989), 231–39.

4. James I and VI, Speech of March 29, 1603, in McIlwain, op. cit., 269.

5. Ibid., 280.

6. Sir Edward Coke, "Speech in Prosecution of Henry Garnet," in W. J. Adams, *The Gunpowder Treason* (London, 1851), 163.

7. Caesar "Jesuitically" defends his murder of Candy as done for the man's own good (2085–87):

> He was an honest man, and fit for heaven.
> Whils't he liv'd here, he breathed in misery
> And would have been enlarg'd—I set him free.

8. T. F. Wharton, *Moral Experiment in Jacobean Drama* (St. Martin's Press, 1988).

9. Compare the description of Barnes's evil Pope: "Ambitious, avaricious, shameless, devilish" (line 1120).

10. Garnet, in his *Treatise of Equivocation*, said that legitimate equivocation is controlled truth not outright lying. If it were used outside the rules he prescribes, that would make people "more inconstant than Proteus, more variable than the chameleon, more deceitful than Sinon" (Jardine edition, 54). Though these were,

taken singly, conventional comparisons, the cluster of those three examples and no others suggests that Garnet saw *Richard III,*, popular in the period near Southwell's death (1595). The 1595 Quarto has the chameleon and Proteus but not Sinon. *See* Michael J. B. Allen and Kenneth Muir, *Shakespeare's Plays in Quarto* (University of California Press, 1981), 101.

11. Geoffrey Bullough, *Narrative and Dramatic Sources of Shakespeare*, Vol. 7, (Routledge and Kegan Paul, 1973), 502–3.

12. H. L. Rogers, *"Double Profit" in Macbeth* (Melbourne University Press, 1964), 11.

13. See Chapter One, note 43.

14. For Jonson's deception of a woman fond of astrology by meeting her "disguised in a long cloak," see "Conversations with Drummond," in C. H. Herford and Percy Simpson, *Ben Jonson: Works* (Oxford University Press, 1925), Vol. 1, p. 141.

15. The "with him" calls for a slight change of F's antecedent, *med'cine*, to *med'c'ner*, a less wrenching change than the supposed one that makes *medicine* mean *physician*.

16. H. N. Paul usefully quotes from King James's *Counter-Blaste to Tobacco* (1604): "It is the king's part, as the proper physician of his politic body, to purge it of all those diseases by medicines meet for the same." Paul, *The Royal Play of Macbeth* (Octagon Books reprint, 1978), 391.

Seven · Macbeth

1. Defenses of "shoal" get desperate. Brooke writes "reference to the sea [!] springs from the fishing sense of 'trammel.'" But "trammel" was used more of netting animals on land than of netting fish.

2. Cleanth Brooks, *The Well Wrought Urn* (Harcourt Brace Jovanovich, 1947), 22–49.

3. Helen Gardner, *The Business of Criticism* (Oxford University Press, 1959), 53–61.

4. Kenneth Muir, *Aspects of "Macbeth"* (Cambridge University Press, 1977), 66–68.

5. *Johnson on Shakespeare*, edited by Arthur Sherbo (Yale University Press, 1968), Vol. 2, p. 767. Cf. Gardner, op.cit., 59, on "the wind dropping as the rain begins."

Notes

6. It is interesting that all the critics refer to the babe as "he," though the virtues were normally female when personified. Blake, too, made the babe male in his large color print illustrating the passage. For a discussion of Blake's "Pity," see Jonathan Bate, *Shakespeare and the English Romantic Imagination* (Clarendon Press, 1989), 125–27.

7. *The Poems of Robert Southwell, S.J.*, edited by James H. McDonald and Nancy Pollard Brown (Clarendon Press, 1967), 15–16. For date of the poem's publication, see pp. lxv and 124. The text available to Shakespeare in 1602 mistakenly printed "bred" for "fed" at the end of the third stanza. Christopher Devlin argued, on no very good evidence, that Southwell and Shakespeare were friends (*The Life of Robert Southwell*, 1956). But it is likely that Shakespeare knew the Jesuit's poems—there was a vogue for them just after the 1595 execution. It was the eighth edition of his poems in which "The Burning Babe" appeared (in 1602). See McDonald and Brown, op.cit., lv–lxvi.

8. *Two Noble Kinsmen* 2.2.249–50.

9. I suspect that the troupe had at the time a fine costume of armor that fit Burbage, since there is an elaborate arming scene in the contemporary *Antony* 4.4.1–18.

10. Dennis Bartholomeusz, *Macbeth and the Players* (Cambridge University Press, 1969), 260.

11. See David Bevington and Eric Rasmussen, *Doctor Faustus, A and B Texts, 1604, 1616* (Manchester University Press, 1993), 92.

12. Ibid., 49.

13. Line 1134: "Those robes pontifical which thou profaned." Lines 1822–23: "crimes / Lurk underneath the robes of holiness." Line 2077: "Your sins more heinous, yet your robes conceal them." Line 2132: "To cloak my vices I will pardon yours." Lines 2430–31: "your reverend purple robes / Which should protect . . . ."

14. It would have been theatrically effective to have the Whore (who was also the Pope) played by a man—to emphasize his unnatural aspect (the effect Shakespeare achieves with his witches played by men).

15. Rosenberg, 510.

16. Janet Arnold, *Queen Elizabeth's Wardrobe Unlock'd* (W. S. Maney & Son, 1988), 81–84, 92; and *The Raigne of King Edward the Third*, edited by Fred Lapides (Garland Publishing, 1980), lines 707–15. For Shakespeare's possible role in the composition of *Edward III*, see Chapter 4, note 20.

17. George Chapman, *Homer's "Odysses"* 5.66–68. Cf. the similar use of "mis-ease" at 13.139. For the hyphen in dis-ease, see F's "dis-heartens" at *Macbeth* 2.3.33.

18. The two lines preceding make no sense as normally delivered:

> She should have died hereafter,
> There would have been a time for such a word.

Editors take this to mean, "I am too distracted to mourn now. If she died later, I could take in the meaning of that event." But (1) he does not know there will be a later occasion, (2) "There would *have been* a time" seems to look to the past, not the future, and (3) Macbeth goes on to say there will be no special time to be marked in the future (made up of featureless tomorrows) *or* the past (yesterdays lighting fools). If the future and past are ruled out, *only* the present is left as a "time for such a word." But he is saying that *no* time is a right time any more, distinguishable from other times. No *kairos* will exist for him, ever again. Then why does he say, "There would have been a time"? The first two lines must be *questions,* to which the rest of the speech gives a despairing answer:

> She should have died hereafter [in the future]?
> There would have been time for such a word [in the past]?
> ["No" understood]. Tomorrow, and. . . .

19. The Geneva translation of 1560. The Psalms are the part of the Bible most echoed in Shakespeare. Richmond Noble wrote that "there is not a play in the Folio entirely free from a suggestion of a use of the Psalms" (*Shakespeare's Biblical Knowledge* (Octagon Books reprint, 1970), 47).

20. Lucan, *Pharsalia* 6.557–58.

21. Stephen Orgel, editor, *Ben Jonson: The Complete Masques* (Yale University Press, 1969), 535.

22. "I pull in resolution" of F calls for a metrically clumsy emphasis on *in* to get either of the two suggested and contrary meanings ("I inhale *new* resolution," or "I limit my *former* resolution"). Johnson suggested *pall,* but *pale* is as easy a setter's slip, and paling has been a regular theme in the play: "look so green and pale" (1.7.37); "wear a heart so white" (2.2.64); "bond which keeps me pale" (3.2.50); "look not so pale" (5.1.63); "cream-fac'd" (5.3.11); "linen cheeks" (5.3.16); "whey-face" (5.3.17).

Notes

Appendix · I

1. Gary Taylor and John Jowett, *Shakespeare Reshaped, 1606–1623* (Clarendon Press, 1993), 85.

2. Stanley Wells and Gary Taylor, *William Shakespeare: A Textual Companion* (Clarendon Press, 1987), 128–29.

3. F. A. Loomis, "Master of the Tiger," *Shakespeare Quarterly* 7 (1956): 457.

4. H. L. Rogers, "An English Tailor and Father Garnet's Straw," *Review of English Studies*, 1965, 44–49.

5. Francis Beaumont, *The Knight of the Burning Pestle*, edited by Michael Hattaway (Ernest Benn, 1969), 100:

> When thou art at thy table with thy friends,
> Merry in heart and fill'd with swelling wine,
> I'll come in midst of all thy pride and mirth,
> Invisible to all men but thyself,
> And whisper such a sad tale in thine ear
> Shall make thee let the cup fall from thy hand,
> And stand as mute and pale as death itself.

6. Ibid., x–xi.

7. When King Christian returned to England in 1607, the famous bear George Stone was baited to the death (an expensive form of entertainment) in the King's honor. Chambers, *Elizabethan Stage* (Oxford University Press, 1967), Vol. 2, pp. 457–58.

8. The time constraints of entertainment during the royal visit are listed by Leeds Barroll in *Politics, Plague, and Shakespeare's Theater* (Cornell University Press, 1991), 148–49.

9. Ibid., 147.

10. For the dating of *Antony* to the 1606–07 Christmas season, see John Pitcher's views cited in Wells and Taylor, op.cit., 129–30, and Barroll, op. cit., 160–68.

11. Barroll, op. cit., 170–71. Shakespeare's productivity would have been affected not only by his own health, activities, and opportunities, but by his company's vicissitudes of casts, costs, and internal politics.

12. Chambers, op. cit., Vol. 4, p. 139, quotes Walter Cope's January letter to Robert Cecil:

> I have sent and been all this morning hunting for players, jugglers, and such kind of creatures but find them hard to find. Wherefore, leaving notes for them to

seek me, Burbage is come and says there is no new play that the Queen hath not seen, but they have revived an old one called Loves Labor [*sic*] Lost.

If the list in the account of the Master of Revels for the 1604–05 season is authentic, none of the twelve plays Burbage put on at court during the extended Christmas celebrations was new (with the possible exception of *Othello*). For the list, see E. K. Chambers, *William Shakespeare* (Clarendon Press, 1930), Vol. 2, pp. 330–32.

13. Using the TLN (Through Line Numbering) system of the Norton Facsimile, the figures for the shortest plays are: *The Comedy of Errors*, 1,918; *The Tempest*, 2,318; *Macbeth*, 2,528; *Julius Caesar*, 2,730. All the other tragedies are over 3000 lines.

14. The favorite hypothesis for shortened revisions used to be creation of "traveling" editions for playing with reduced numbers in the provinces. That is not in accord with the Hecate scenes' *addition* of players in *Macbeth*. Besides, the whole idea of shortened editions for the provinces has been struck a heavy blow by David Bradley, *From Text to Performance in the Elizabethan Theatre* (Cambridge University Press, 1992), 58–74.

15. W. J. Lawrence went even farther and supposed that Shakespeare's troupe transferred parts of Jonson's masque to *The Witch*, and then to *Macbeth*. See Lawrence, *Shakespeare's Workshop* (Blackwell, 1928), 24–38. It is true that the Hecate scenes share some witch lore with the *Masque's* scenes, but so do Gunpowder plays like *Sophonisba* and *The Whore of Babylon*, performed three years before Jonson's masque.

16. For the need to gain a new license for altered texts, see the defense of the players of *Game at Chess* that they had not "added [to] or varied from" the licensed text. Virginia Crocheron Gildersleeve, *Government Regulation of the Elizabethan Drama* (Columbia University Press, 1908), 120. It was dangerous to play "outside the book" licensed by the Master of Revels. When the King's Men wanted to revive *The Winter's Tale* in 1623, even without revisions, they found they had misplaced the license on their playbook and therefore resubmitted it for a new license, swearing they had made no changes: Joseph Quincy Adams, *The Dramatic Records of Sir Henry Herbert, Master of the Revels, 1623–1673* (Yale University Press, 1917), 25. A new reading, paid for by a new fee, was necessary "for allowing . . . to add scenes to an old play" (ibid., 37). For the need to produce a licensed text for one's performance if challenged, see Bradley, op. cit., 60.

17. A. A. Bromham, "The Date of *The Witch* and the Essex Divorce Case," *Notes and Queries* 225 (1980): 149–52.

Notes

18. Anne Lancashire, *"The Witch*, Stage Flop or Political Mistake?" in *Accompaninge the Players*, edited by Karl Friedenreich (AMS Press, 1983), 161–81.

19. One effect of revision, as I stated earlier, may have been the removal of more blatant references to the Gunpowder Plot. The relaxed censorship of 1606 no longer applied, and the censor may well have taken the attitude Henry Herbert did when asked to relicense Fletcher's *The Loyal Subject*—he granted it only "with some reformations" (J. Q. Adams, op. cit., 35).

Appendix · II

1. See his versions of Matthew 17.16, Romans 1.29, Habakkuk 1.4, Ecclesiasticus 27.26, Matthew 6.23.

2. Of children, *Love's Labour's* 3.1.179, *Romeo* 4.2.47, *Venus* 344. Of illness, *Richard II* 2.1.142, *Richard III* 1.3.29, 4.4.169, *Lear* 1.1.298.

3. William Empson, *Seven Types of Ambiguity*, revised edition (New Directions, 1966), 45.

4. Modern editors can miss Shakespeare's regular punning on "tell" and "tale" as *counting* language. When Borachio and Conrade are accused of being knaves, and Borachio says "we are none," Dogberry takes "none" numerically and answers "they are *both* in a *tale* [count]," so how can they be "none"? (*Much Ado* 4.2.29–31). Earlier, when Benedict (as a lover) is crept into a lute, to be governed by stops, "that tells a heavy tale for him" (makes a heavy count in his music, 3.2.59–62). The uses that have shrunk, in our day, to linguistic remnants like bank *teller*, or *tell* time were omnipresent in Shakespeare's day.

5. The Rowe emendation of *tale/can* to *hail/came*, commonly accepted, shows how little palaeographical procedure is regarded in the attempt to wrest meaning from this passage. I change nothing in the text but orthography, since *afear'd* and *affeer'd* are homophones variously spelled.

Line Index to the Play

Line Index to the Play

Line Index to the Play

Name Index

Adelman, Janet, 179n32
Aeneid (Vergil), 181n6
Ajax (fictional character), 182n14
The Alchemist (Jonson), 185n33
Alexander VI, Pope (as dramatic
  character): character description
  of, 196n9; clothes of, 137–38;
  and confusion, 173n43; contract
  of, 25, 36, 46, 172n31; and
  equivocation/language, 25, 113;
  and homosexuality, 175n6; Lucretia's relationship with, 83; repentance of, 89, 141; and
  witchcraft, 36, 37, 42–43, 47,
  66, 67–68, 74, 79, 143, 175n6,
  184n24, 190n18
Alleyn, Richard, 137
All's Well That Ends Well (Shakespeare), 183n22, 194n15
Amphion (fictional character), 78
Andrewes, Lancelot: answers
  Bellarmino, 173n47; and darkness, 54–55; and the horrors of
  the plot, 24, 25, 171–72n28; and
  language, 172n38, 172n40; and

the official interpretation of the
  plot, 17, 23–24; and undermining of the plot, 24, 30; and
  witchcraft, 36, 37, 54–55
Angus (fictional character), 139
Antony and Cleopatra (Shakespeare):
  arming scene in, 198n9; and
  darkness, 66, 184n25; and dating
  of *Macbeth*, 151, 152, 153–54;
  early performances of, 78, 151,
  152, 153–54; and witchcraft, 66,
  188n10, 190n20. *See also*
  Cleopatra (as dramatic character)
Armin, Robert, 86, 98, 102, 105,
  190n27
Asnath (devil in drama), 45, 47
Autolycus (fictional character),
  162

Banquo (as dramatic character):
  and the banquet scene, 71–72;
  and darkness/light, 57, 58, 59,
  60, 62; and equivocation/
  language, 142; ghost of, 186n38;